BEING AN
Effective
MENTOR

In loving memory of my father,
Raymond Lloyd Feeney
1921-2002

Master tradesman;
Mentor to scores of apprentices.

BEING AN
Effective
MENTOR

How to
Help
Beginning
Teachers
Succeed

Kathleen Feeney JONSON

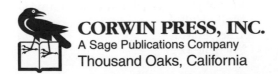

CORWIN PRESS, INC.
A Sage Publications Company
Thousand Oaks, California

For information:

Corwin Press, Inc.
A Sage Publications Company
2455 Teller Road
Thousand Oaks, California 91320
www.corwinpress.com

Sage Publications Ltd.
6 Bonhill Street
London EC2A 4PU

United Kingdom
Sage Publications India Pvt. Ltd.
M-32 Market
Greater Kailash I
New Delhi 110 048 India

Printed in the United States of America

Library of Congress Cataloging-in-Publication Data

Jonson, Kathleen Feeney.
   Being an effective mentor: How to help beginning teachers succeed / by Kathleen Feeney Jonson.
       p. cm.
Includes bibliographical references and index.
   ISBN 0-7619-4524-5 (c) -- ISBN 0-7619-4549-0 (p)
 1. Mentoring in education--United States--Handbooks, manuals, etc. 2. First year teachers--Training of--United States--Handbooks, manuals, etc. I. Title.
   LB1731.4 .J66 2002
   371.102--dc21

                              2001007405

              06 07 6

This book is printed on acid-free paper.

Acquisitions Editor:	Rachel Livsey
Editorial Assistant:	Phyllis Cappello
Production Editor:	Olivia Weber
Typesetter/Designer:	Larry K. Bramble
Copy Editors:	Rachel Hile Bassett and Linda Gray
Indexer:	Molly Hall
Cover Designer:	Tracy E. Miller
Production Artist:	Michelle Lee

Contents

Preface

Has there been anyone in your personal or professional life to whom you've regularly turned for advice and support? Someone who has had a significant and positive impact on your career as an educator? A caring coworker you might even call your "mentor"?

Many veteran teachers were never actually assigned a mentor. If they were lucky, they found informal assistance from experienced coworkers. Many think back to their first year in the classroom and remember the confusion of a difficult and lonely time during which no one came to their aid.

Fortunately, times are changing. Policies to establish teacher mentoring programs are currently sweeping the nation. At this writing, 28 states and the District of Columbia have instituted formal, state-funded and mandated mentoring programs. Of course, even today, not all beginning teachers are fortunate enough to get the support they may need, but it is certainly a step in the right direction that someone like you is reading this book.

Mentoring programs attract caring and committed teachers who recognize the complex and challenging nature of classroom teaching. In mentoring, these teachers demonstrate their hope and optimism for the future. They "pass the torch" by helping a new teacher become effective. They hope the beginner will discover the joys and satisfactions that they have found in their own careers. Mentors are not naive Pollyannas, however. They understand that mentoring can be a challenging endeavor requiring significant investments of time and energy. They have lots of empathy, but their decision to help is grounded in the real and the practical.

Mentoring is defined as the professional practice that provides support, assistance, and guidance to beginning teachers to promote their professional growth and success. It is sometimes one program within a larger teacher induction program that also includes other activities such as orientations and inservices. The mentoring component is usually a one-on-

one relationship. A mentor can serve as a friend, guide, counselor, supporter, and teacher.

In a complex and demanding profession such as teaching, there's no substitute for experience and a repertoire of "tried and true" strategies. Many beginning teachers find the stressful reality of their own classroom to be a shock. They struggle to cope. These new teachers—and their students—deserve the support and guidance of a skilled and experienced mentor.

This book focuses on helping mentors develop effective mentoring strategies. Chapters 1 and 2 provide a knowledge base to structure the development of a mentoring program. These introductory chapters contain a historical and policy perspective. In this sense, they are particularly important for staff developers, program administrators, and teacher leaders. They will provide teachers and administrators with an understanding of the underlying principles and prerequisites of successful mentoring programs. Topics explored include the role of the mentor, qualifications of a good mentor, and the importance of providing preparation and support for the mentoring process.

In Chapter 3, mentors are encouraged to remember their own first days in the classroom as they prepare to work with their new teachers. "Reality shock" and the fears and anxieties of beginners are discussed. Chapter 4 overviews the myriad of skills the beginner needs to get off to a good start: teaching skills, interpersonal skills, and coping skills. Helping the beginner acquire these skills requires that the mentor perform a variety of functions. These functions range from serving as a role model in the full scope of daily professional activities to developing specific skills such as classroom observation. In Chapter 5, therefore, we turn to specific strategies for mentoring, including direct assistance, demonstration teaching, observation and feedback, informal contact, and role modeling. How mentors use these techniques to develop trusting relationships is the heart of Chapter 6, "Working as a Partner With the Adult Learner." Because mentoring relationships go through phases, Chapter 6 deals with how mentors need to adjust their responses as their protégés develop. Reflection is encouraged as an activity to promote refinement and discovery.

Chapter 7 asks the important question "Why be a mentor?" and takes a close look at the pitfalls and payoffs. There is little doubt that ongoing, meaningful contact between mentors and protégés reinforces and fosters professional development and builds trust. Chapter 8 offers a month-by-month listing of suggested activities designed to promote interaction between mentors and protégés. Activities have been suggested for each month to correspond with typical activities and events occurring in a school year. Finally, five appendixes provide valuable information and tools to help the mentor work with the beginning teacher.

Although intended primarily for mentors, this book will be of interest to anyone concerned with the complex process of guidance, assistance, and support to promote growth and success for beginning teachers. Principals, staff developers, university supervisors, beginning and experienced teachers, even parents and community members—we all can benefit from an understanding of the value and process of mentoring.

ACKNOWLEDGMENTS

The contributions of the following reviewers are gratefully acknowledged:

Patricia Schwartz
Principal
Thomas Jefferson Middle School
Teaneck, New Jersey

Joan Roberts
Coordinator/Administrator
Monterey County Office of
  Education
Salinas, California

RoseAnne O'Brien Vojtek
Principal
Ivy Drive Elementary School
Bristol Public Schools
Bristol, Connecticut

Linda Munger
Educational Consultant
Munger Education Associates
Des Moines, Iowa

Marti Richardson
NSDC Board of Trustees
Staff Development Supervisor
Knoxville, Tennessee

About the Author

Kathleen Feeney Jonson, Ed.D., is currently Associate Professor and Coordinator of the Multiple Subject Credential Program in the Teacher Education Department of the University of San Francisco. As the oldest of nine children, she says she was born to teach and mentor! In her 32 years as an educator, she has taught at the elementary and secondary levels and has served as a reading specialist, director of staff development, principal, and director of curriculum and instruction. She has conducted numerous workshops for teachers and administrators on such topics as integrating the curriculum, reading comprehension strategies, writing process, portfolio assessment, peer coaching, and beginning teacher assistance programs. She has developed numerous curriculum guides, training syllabi, and program materials for educators and parents. Her professional experience includes teaching university courses in elementary and secondary curriculum and instruction, as well as serving as Field Coordinator working with student teachers, mentor teachers, and university supervisors. The second edition of her book *The New Elementary Teacher's Handbook* (1997) was published by Corwin Press in 2001.

1

Passing the Torch

Those having torches will pass them on to others.

—Plato, *The Republic*

Twenty second graders stand in line inside the door to room 3D at Lincoln Elementary School. "Kyle cut!" Cameron insists, gripping his folder and lunch box. Ms. Blackwell glances at the boys, but Kyle denies the accusation. The clock ticks to 2:40 p.m., and the bell rings. With a weary smile, Ms. Blackwell waves good-bye and watches as the children scurry out, the two boys still arguing. Feeling a sense of relief, she turns back into the classroom. Too late, she discovers that Caitlin has forgotten to put her chair up on her table again, and Danny hasn't picked up his pencil from the floor as she asked him to do. She must work on better follow-through.

Ms. Blackwell kneels to pick up Danny's pencil, lifts up Caitlin's chair, and returns to her desk. Sighing, she looks at the pile of spelling papers on her desk, the large, dark letters carefully—or not so carefully—printed on wide lines. With a glance, she can tell that most of the words on the top paper are misspelled. She had been so sure that her new study-in-buddies idea would work, but apparently it hadn't. At least not for everyone.

Ms. Blackwell sets aside the papers, too disheartened to review them. Her eyes burn as she reflects on her day. Again today, Maggie complained that James was chasing her on the playground. The experiment Ms. Blackwell had planned for the unit on rocks was too difficult. And her throat is burning—but she can't take time off and leave her class with a substitute. She looks at her desk. Oh. And there's that form she was supposed to have returned to the office yesterday. She should take care of that now—except that she doesn't really understand it. Besides, she needs to get to a teachers' meeting by 3:00. She was late to the last one. Better be on time for this one. Don't want to appear unable to manage.

Ms. Blackwell plants the late form in the middle of her desk so she will be sure to see it first thing when she returns, gathers her papers for the meeting, grabs a tissue for her runny nose, and heads out into the hall. She wonders if any of the other new teachers have these problems or if it's just her.

She had done so well at the university, had loved student teaching with Mr. Beverly. What had happened? Would it ever get easier? She had worked so hard last August to set up her classroom perfectly, tacking up colorful wall coverings and organizing things as discussed in her university classes. Everyone—her professors and friends and the people at Mr. Beverly's school—had assured her that she would make a great teacher. But she doesn't seem to be doing so well now. She tries to think about how Mr. Beverly might handle James. But the boys in Mr. Beverly's fourth grade hadn't chased the girls. Seems that few of the problems she faces now came up when she student-taught with Mr. Beverly. If only she had a Mr. Beverly to turn to now.

The anxieties and frustrations that Ms. Blackwell feels are typical of first-year teachers—and sometimes of teachers in general. No matter how well prepared a beginning teacher may be upon entering the profession—no matter how positive her preservice experience—the early years are always difficult. Issues of classroom and time management commonly cause significant stress. Tasks to be completed seem endless, and when a problem arises, the teacher, alone in the classroom, cannot turn to a coworker for immediate support as another professional in another field might do. Too often during the first years of on-the-job training, teachers throughout history have had to master their craft by trial and error, in an isolated environment, with little feedback.

The first two years of teaching are particularly critical. During this time, the teacher builds the foundation for a satisfying and productive career. But these first two years are also considered by many to be the hardest. In this profession, unlike in others, the beginning teacher has the same workload and responsibilities as the veteran. There is no period for adjustment. What might seem to be the simple mechanics of running a real-world classroom from day to day prove to be surprisingly distressing and stressful.

The result? Often during this "induction" period, beginning teachers feel overwhelmed. Many soon become frustrated and eager to leave. Far too many report lying awake, unable to sleep at night, fretting about their students and school responsibilities. According to a recent survey, teachers (followed by nurses, accountants, and newspaper reporters) are the people most likely to report losing sleep over work-related worries ("Losing Sleep," 2001). This beginning teacher sheds some light on the problem:

> Stress! You're teaching classes all day long. You're keeping students on task, you're testing, you're trying to follow all the rules—every principle and guideline that's set out for you. You're adhering to a schedule: you must teach all the things in the course of study by the end of the year. After school you go home and take your job with you. Then you must face kids who have homework and a husband who has had a tough day, too. (quoted in Gordon & Maxey, 2000, p. 66)

To many in their first year of teaching, then, figuring out how to control students whose first instincts are anything but cooperative makes just surviving a real accomplishment. Without assistance and support, these beginning teachers burn out early at a high rate. Some, overwhelmed by all the "juggling" they have to do, leave the teaching profession altogether. Nationwide, in fact, 30% of beginning teachers leave the profession within two years; another 10% leave after three years; and more than half leave within five to seven years (Pearson & Honig, 1992, p. 5). In urban districts, attrition occurs even faster: Half the teachers are gone within three years (Haberman, 1987; Zimpher & Grossman, 1992, p. 141).

Particularly disturbing are the findings of an in-depth study indicating that the most academically proficient teachers are also the most likely to leave the field (Schlechty & Vance, 1983; Smith, 1993, p. 6). In a study of beginning teachers within San Diego County, California, a teacher leaving the profession after her first year had received one of only six National Education Outstanding Student Teacher Awards given in 1988 (Mathison, 1996, p. 15). The loss of such a potentially exceptional teacher clearly indicates that something is wrong.

Why would someone who had spent four to six years preparing for a profession leave the career within a year or two? What is it that makes beginning teacher after beginning teacher feel as if his years of study have left him unprepared for the world of teaching? And how can this situation be changed to benefit the children in U.S. classrooms?

ENTER THE MENTOR

Throughout the United States, educational systems began to realize in the early 1980s that a serious problem existed: Teachers need assistance and guidance, especially during their early years in the profession. No matter how well prepared, a teacher like Ms. Blackwell needs someone to turn to with the inevitable questions and problems that arise as she begins her profession in the classroom. With this recognition, more than 30 states now mandate support for beginning teachers as part of their teacher induction programs (Portner, 1998, p. 3). Increasingly, school districts are arranging for experienced teachers (*mentors*) to guide these beginning teachers (*mentees,* or *protégés*) through the difficult early years.

Although this book focuses on support for beginning teachers, it is important to note that new-to-the-system teachers also often need assistance (Smith, 1993, p. 7). In some locations, mentors have been recruited to work not only with beginning teachers but also with teachers new to the district or even with experienced teachers having difficulty. Both groups of teachers need practical assistance with things such as schedules for breaks and for lunch, hall, and yard duty, and information about where to get supplies and materials, about required forms and meetings, and so on. Like newcomers to the profession, veterans moving to a different location need a realistic view of their new school to help them "understand the challenges that inevitably surface when people experience the transition from one job to another" (Gordon & Maxey, 2000, p. 84). Mentors can help the newcomer understand the culture and philosophy of the school and can provide the emotional and intellectual support needed in the early days and months of adjustment.

The idea of a mentor to help a beginner is certainly nothing new. The term *mentor* itself dates back to the eighth or ninth century B.C., specifically to Homer's *Odyssey.* In his epic poem, Homer describes his hero, Odysseus, as Odysseus prepares to set out on a 10-year voyage. Odysseus must leave behind his son, Telemachus, and asks his trusted friend Mentor to guide and counsel Telemachus in his absence. While the father is gone, Mentor serves as a sage adviser to the younger man, helping him to grow intellectually, emotionally, and socially. From this ancient literary figure, *mentor* has come to refer to a wise and faithful counselor who helps to guide a protégé through a developmental process. This could be the process of transition from youth to adulthood, as in the case of Telemachus, or from student to professional, as with a first-year teacher.

Modern-day mentors are found in many segments of society. The Big Brother and Big Sister programs are based on the mentor concept: Responsible adults are paired with children; they build a trusting relationship with those children and share with them a variety of activities, guiding them as they grow into young adults. Athletic or drama coaches could also be considered mentors, directing novices in their field. In the professional arena, doctors and lawyers have long been mentored through internship programs, and plumbers, printers, and other skilled tradespeople serve in apprenticeships, another variation of mentorships.

As these examples illustrate, the skills involved, age groups, and degree of formality vary widely among mentoring programs. The common thread, though, is that all such programs are based on a trusting relationship between an experienced adult and a novice. In each case, the organization or business that wants to retain and develop its members provides some sort of mentor support. The idea is not for the mentor to evaluate or judge the protégé, but rather for the mentee to receive guidance. The mentor is defined more by relationship with a beginner than by a position or title.

Some such relationships happen spontaneously: A new employee asks advice of a more experienced colleague, who sees potential in the beginner and continues to offer support. Other pairings result from a considered design. Large corporations, for example, sometimes match senior managers to ambitious, talented junior employees. The mentor in this situation may help the newer employee with issues such as balancing personal and business lives, as well as working within the corporate environment. The mentee learns that her concerns are not unique—that other employees have experienced the same problems—and this knowledge helps her grow professionally.

According to several studies, mentors have played an important role in the career development of many highly successful people in business. In one study, researchers found that businesspeople who had mentors earned more money at a younger age and were more satisfied with their work and career advancement than were those without mentors (Bolton, 1980; Odell, 1990, p. 5; Roche, 1979). Mentoring programs in business were found to help the protégé with personal adjustment, satisfaction, and professional achievement (Bova, 1987; Cohen, 1995, p. 4; Kram, 1985; Marsick, 1987; Zey, 1984). In both university and business settings, protégés of mentors learned risk-taking behaviors, communication skills, political skills, and specific skills that helped them in their professions (Bova & Phillips, 1983; Odell, 1990, p. 6). Even in government, mentors have helped employees develop their careers and prepare for senior positions (Cohen, 1995, p. 4; Murray, 1991).

Mentoring would seem to be a natural progression in the teaching profession, too, where experienced teachers have traditionally passed on their expertise and wisdom to new colleagues. For a beginning teacher, clearly, the benefits of working closely with a mentor are great, no matter how extensive the preservice education. Beginning teachers are faced by and accountable for (or to—it is not always clear which) an array of unknown students, teaching colleagues, administrators, and parents. As Ms. Blackwell discovered, even routine paperwork can be overwhelming when the teacher does not understand it and does not know where to look for help. In addition, school and community environments have norms and rituals that are probably new and obscure to a newcomer. The large number of actual and procedural unknowns can send the beginning teacher into a state of shock wherein it becomes impossible to transfer previously mastered concepts and skills from the university to the K-12 classroom. Ms. Blackwell could have benefited greatly from the help of a veteran teacher familiar with her grade level and school site.

So far in education, relatively little hard research has been conducted on the effects of mentoring. Many descriptive studies and program evaluations clearly conclude, however, that a good mentor-mentee relationship significantly benefits the beginning teacher, not only during the difficult first year but also in years to come. Through an examination of the literature and many research studies on beginning teachers, Varah, Theune, and Parker (1986) have concluded that "collaborative teacher induction programs are effective means of strengthening beginning teacher performance" (quoted in Smith, 1993, p. 6). Other studies have also indicated that mentors and induction programs are overwhelmingly successful, increasing the retention of beginning teachers and ameliorating first-year difficulties (Bey, 1992, p. 114; Smith, 1993).

Despite this seemingly natural form of assistance, teachers have had no formal system like those used in businesses through which to receive guidance once they entered their first professional classroom—until recently. Not until the early 1980s did those in the teaching profession begin to take up the torch. Now the trend is gaining momentum, however. In 1997, the U.S. Secretary of Education included in his initiatives, published in *The Seven Priorities of the U.S. Department of Education*, "special efforts to retain beginning teachers in their first few years of teaching" (U.S. Department of Education, 1997). That same year, in his *Call to Action of American Education in the 21st Century*, then-President Bill Clinton announced that school districts must "make sure that beginning teachers get support and mentoring from experienced teachers" (*President Clinton's Call*, 1997). With an estimated 2 million-plus beginning teachers needed to replace retirees and accommodate growing numbers of students within the next decade (Association for Supervision and Curriculum Development [ASCD], 1999c, p. 1; Portner, 1998, p. 4), it is increasingly important to guide and retain those entering the profession. (More recently, President George W. Bush has focused on standards and testing.)

Teachers themselves support the idea of teacher-mentors. Teachers have reported that they get their best innovative ideas regarding teaching from other teachers (Sergiovanni, 1992, p. 86). In one large national study funded by Public Agenda, many administrators and new teachers expressed a belief that mentoring programs could significantly improve teacher quality (Farkas, Johnson, & Foleno, 2000, p. 29). In another national sample, this one looking at 1,007 beginning teachers, 46% said an experienced teacher assigned to advise and assist them would have been most helpful in preparing them to become more effective as first-year teachers (Bey, 1992, p. 111; Lou Harris & Associates, 1991).

THE ROLE OF THE TEACHER-MENTOR

In the field of teaching, the mentor plays a vital and unique role in the development and training of someone new to the profession. An effective mentor provides support and collegiality, alleviating the isolation so often experienced by the beginning teacher. What makes the mentor different from others who may help is that the mentor develops a relationship of trust with the beginning teacher over an extended period of time and remains with the mentee as he evolves and as issues develop. One California mentor notes that this is particularly important: "My mentee and I have a trusting relationship in that he can be open and honest with his needs." In contrast, a principal, for example, may be available to help with a specific, one-time problem on a practical level but does not necessarily provide ongoing, daily help with a range of emotional, curricular, and instructional questions.

For a variety of reasons, an experienced colleague is particularly suited to the mentor role. Because the colleague is close at hand, she is available when the mentee needs guidance, in both formal and informal contexts. Both parties work in the same setting and with similar goals, so they can often relate to each other's experiences; Ms. Blackwell, for example, might have found help from a mentor who had shared her problems with the students at her school. Because integrity and trust are vital to a good mentor-mentee relationship, many experienced mentors feel strongly that mentors should not be involved in evaluating their mentees. If this is the case, the mentee is more likely to share experiences, fears, and concerns without the anxiety of being judged. This same beginning teacher might be reluctant to share these feelings or problems with a principal, for example, who will later evaluate her and help make decisions about the future of her career.

The primary task of the mentor, then, is to establish a relationship with the beginning teacher based on mutual trust, respect, and collegiality. Through the sharing of frustrations and successes, the beginning teacher learns that problems are normal, and this helps build confidence. One California mentor believes that important contributions for a mentee might include "validating the challenges of teaching; taking [the mentees'] ideas and feelings seriously; helping them to trust their own judgment." Another points out the value of "discussing problems realistically and letting them know I have the same problems sometimes; just letting them vent."

Support and encouragement from an effective mentor can thus greatly benefit the beginning teacher. However, in most beginner assistance programs, the mentor also directly assists the beginning teacher, helping him to learn quickly as he is immersed in the complex art and science of teaching. "When I first visited my mentee," one California mentor recalls, "his classroom was completely out of control. Afterward I gave him feedback and five simple, concrete policy suggestions. Immediate implementation led to immediate results." Yet another mentor tells about helping with a specific lesson. "My mentee was having trouble organizing a weather unit," this one said. "So we took a couple of hours and we went through my whole weather file and we made a schedule and lesson plan for the new unit."

Among the mentor's goals, then, should be to help the beginning teacher develop and enhance the following attributes:

- Competence: mastery of the knowledge, skills, and applications that effective teaching requires

- Self-confidence: belief in one's ability to make good decisions, to be responsible, and to be in control

- Self-direction: the assurance and ability to take charge of one's personal, professional, and career development

- Professionalism: an understanding and assumption of the responsibilities and ethics of the profession

Box 1.1 lists five goals for teacher induction programs.

Box 1.1

Teacher Induction Program Goals

Five commonly accepted goals of teacher induction programs, as identified by Huling-Austin (1988), are these:

1. To improve teaching performance

2. To increase retention of promising beginning teachers

3. To promote the personal and professional well-being of beginning teachers

4. To transmit the culture of the system to beginning teachers

5. To satisfy mandated requirements related to induction and certifications

THE GOOD MENTOR: WHAT DOES IT TAKE?

The task of mentoring is complex and requires the skills of a teacher, counselor, friend, role model, guide, sponsor, coach, resource, and colleague. Through the years, mentors have also gone by the names of *host, supporter, adviser, positive role model, confidant, guru, master teacher, teacher adviser, teacher specialist, colleague teacher, peer teacher,* and *support teacher.*

Under any name, though, the idea is the same: An experienced and expert professional develops a relationship with a trained but inexperienced protégé. The mentor may incorporate a variety of strategies and activities to help the protégé grow and develop in professional competence, attitudes, and behaviors—but regardless of the specific activities and goals, the qualitative nature of the relationship determines the overall effectiveness of the mentor.

So what makes a good mentor? Is it just a matter of being a highly accomplished teacher? Certainly that's a good starting point, but it's not enough. Commitment to promoting excellence in the teaching profession? That's important, too. But even more is required. Mentors are special people. Good ones have qualities and responsibilities that include but go beyond those of a good teacher. For teachers, a good mentor

- Is a skilled teacher

- Is able to transmit effective teaching strategies

- Has a thorough command of the curriculum being taught

- Can communicate openly with the beginning teacher

- Is a good listener

- Is sensitive to the needs of the beginning teacher

- Understands that teachers may be effective using a variety of styles

- Is not overly judgmental

Studies show that other desirable qualities in a mentor include wisdom, caring, humor, nurturing, and commitment to the profession (Hardcastle, 1988; Kay, 1990; Odell, 1990, p. 11). If the job were to be posted, an announcement might read something like Box 1.2.

Requirements for mentoring go even beyond these general characteristics and qualities. A good mentor understands the needs of beginning teachers and the stages of teacher development (Chapters 3 and 4). He is armed with effective instructional coaching strategies appropriate for the adult learner (Chapters 5 and 6). Problem-solving skills and the ability to think critically and reflectively are also prerequisites.

Box 1.2.

Job Announcement
Mentor Teacher

Description
Experienced teachers who have mastered their craft and who are dedicated to promoting excellence in the teaching profession are sought as mentors for beginning teachers just starting their careers. Mentors must play several roles, including guide, role model, sponsor, counselor, coach, resource, and colleague.

Responsibilities
As a mentor, you will be responsible for
- Meeting regularly with your protégé, both formally and informally
- Guiding your protégé through the daily operation of the school
- Arranging for your protégé to visit different teachers' classes
- Demonstrating lessons for your protégé
- Observing your protégé's teaching and providing feedback
- Being a role model in all aspects of professionalism
- Developing your skills as a mentor as well as a teacher
- Supporting and counseling your protégé, providing perspective when needed

Qualifications
It takes a special person to be a good mentor. Maturity, self-assurance, patience, and confidence in your knowledge and ability are prerequisites for this important undertaking. More specifically, a good mentor is a teacher who
- Is a skillful teacher
- Is able to transmit effective teaching strategies
- Has a thorough command of the curriculum being taught
- Is a good listener
- Can communicate openly with the beginning teacher
- Is sensitive to the needs of the beginning teacher
- Understands that teachers may be effective using a variety of styles
- Is careful not to be overly judgmental

Conditions of Employment
Extra time, effort, and commitment are required. Increased contact with colleagues, professional stimulation, and sense of accomplishment are likely. Tangible compensation—never enough; intangible rewards—priceless.

Mentors needed every year! Apply now!

Mentoring requires commitment and a willingness to extend oneself for another person. Good mentors must be conscious that their own professional development serves as a model for the beginning teacher and that lifelong learning is as much an attitude as it is an activity; for true professionals, learning is a way of life. With an effective program, the rewards include not only the satisfaction of helping a beginning teacher succeed but also personal and professional growth for the mentor.

> Being a mentor keeps me current. When I have to answer my mentee's questions, it makes me ask, "Why am I doing what I'm doing?" In discussing philosophy, problems, or techniques with this new teacher, I find out what I really believe. That makes me a stronger person and a better teacher. (A beginning teacher's mentor quoted in Gordon & Maxey, 2000, p. 66)

CONCLUSION

This book is intended to provide the rationale and guidelines for setting up an effective mentoring program as well as practical information and advice for new mentors. Chapter 1 has explained for those developing programs why such programs are essential. The mentor plays an especially important role in helping the beginning teacher adjust to a new profession, but a mentor can also be of assistance to a veteran teacher new to a particular setting. In the next chapter, several successful programs will be reviewed and their common elements discussed.

The following chapters will give guidance for the mentor in her new role, reminding her what it was like to be a beginning teacher (Chapter 3) and what basic skills are required of every teacher (Chapter 4). Chapter 5 gives concrete strategies for working with beginning teachers, and Chapter 6 discusses more general aspects of working with adult learners. Chapter 7 asks the question, Why be a mentor anyway? It outlines some of the challenges of the position but also specifies rewards to look forward to. Finally, Chapter 8 includes practical aids for approaching the challenge of helping a beginning teacher adjust to a difficult but rewarding career.

> If teaching is ever to be a profession in the sense that medicine and law are, beginning teachers need a chance to learn what constitutes good practice with the help of accomplished colleagues instead of being forced to figure everything out for themselves. (Shanker, 1995)

2

Setting Up for Success

Dolores sits before a group of young children in her elementary school classroom. Until recently, she worked as an executive for a large corporation. Now she is making the transition to a new profession.

Nancy, a veteran teacher, is in the back of the classroom taking notes as Dolores engages her young students in a round of "Wheels on the Bus." Later, the children remain attentive as their teacher reads aloud to them from a picture book.

After the children have left, Nancy and Dolores sit together at a table in the classroom to discuss the events of the day. Nancy points out that the children were involved in the movements of the opening song and suggests that Dolores help them create movements to go along with the pages of the book as well. She comments on the beginning teacher's method for getting attention (a hand signal using a countdown on fingers) and says with enthusiasm that she plans to try the method in her own classroom the next day.

The two teachers laugh at times as they converse, comfortable with each other, sharing ideas. The mood is friendly and receptive, and it is clear that even two good teachers—both the mentor and the mentee—can become stronger teachers through their relationship.

—Summary from the video Mentoring to Improve Schools *(ASCD, 1999b)*

Dolores and Nancy are teachers in a school district of Fairfax County, Virginia. Fairfax is only one of many districts throughout the United States that have implemented mentoring programs for their beginning teachers during the past two decades. Individual programs vary in the details of how they are set up, but all have been established to help beginning teachers survive the initial shock of teaching reality and progress to become quality educators. Following are examples of four successful programs. After these programs are described, common elements and variations will be discussed.

In Fairfax County, Virginia, every beginning teacher or teacher new to a school automatically participates in a three-year program in which the beginning teacher is paired with a veteran teacher. These veteran teachers, or mentors, work with the assistance of a program coordinator—a sort of mentor's mentor—who does everything from helping to pair the mentor with mentees to coaching mentors to providing other types of support.

The idea is that the veteran teacher will help the novice learn about the school environment and philosophy, become familiar with the curriculum, and understand district procedures and goals. In the scenario at the beginning of this chapter, for example, Nancy helped Dolores with her curriculum. Ultimately, the goals in the Fairfax program are to (a) improve teaching, (b) enhance administrative practices, and (c) create a learning community. In the first year of the program, the focus is on helping the beginning teacher survive. In the second year, the mentor helps the beginning teacher to reflect on his or her own work. By the third year, the beginning teacher suggests topics that he or she is concerned about and would like to work on.

In addition to working with a mentor, beginning teachers in Fairfax County attend weekly meetings where they work on their teaching skills and gain additional support. Alternating meetings are for teaching the participants, who include only beginning and new teachers during these weeks. Off-weeks, for reflection on the previous week's discussion, are open to experienced teachers as well. As the teachers work together, they become stronger and are better able to help the children.

The school system of Minneapolis, Minnesota, uses a different variation on the mentor process (ASCD, 1999b). There, too, beginning teachers work with mentors over a three-year period. There, however, the experienced teacher works as a full-time mentor, relieved from all other teaching responsibilities for the period of the mentorship. Teachers in the system like it because it allows them to develop their mentoring relationships and spend more time in their mentor-mentee pairs.

In the Minneapolis system, unlike in most others, the mentor takes part in evaluating the beginning teacher and in making the decision whether to retain the teacher—but only after the third year. Although most experts agree that mentors should *not* be involved in evaluating their protégés, mentors in this district say it works in their case and may be a fairer way of evaluating a beginning teacher than having an assessment performed by another individual who doesn't have the time required to fully understand a situation.

In yet another state, Kentucky mandated in 1985 the formation of the Kentucky Teacher Internship Program. In this program, a collegial team helps to induct all beginning teaching professionals within the state (Brennan, Thames, & Roberts, 1999, p. 49). In Kentucky, new teachers receive structured assistance and assessment from a committee that includes not only a mentor-teacher but also a university representative and the school principal. The program includes conferences, committee meetings, and 50 hours of paid mentor time with the mentee. Committee members use observations and portfolios to assess the beginning teacher's professional progress. During the first two years of a teacher's induction, assessment is formative, or advisory. During the third year, it is used as a basis for permanent certification.

In California, beginning teachers are supported and encouraged through the Beginning Teacher Support and Assessment (BTSA) program, funded by the state since 1992. BTSA began as the California New Teacher Project, a research program conducted from 1988 to 1992 that examined alternative strategies for supporting and assessing beginning teachers. The program involves on-site coaching, meetings of beginning teachers with support providers, grade-level support seminars, release time for professional growth, funds for supplies, field-based coursework, access to district professional development programs, and training of administrators. BTSA has become a hugely successful program and serves as a model for programs being developed in other states.

Districts within the state of California have set up programs under BTSA in different ways. In the San Francisco Unified School District, the program involves not only the school district but also the teacher education departments of the University of San Francisco and San Francisco State University. The idea is to bridge the knowledge and skills from preservice education to on-the-job experience.

In San Francisco, a school district mentor, or support provider, is assigned to each beginning teacher. The mentor assists and guides beginning teachers but does not evaluate them. One second-year teacher who benefited from the program her second year but not her first wrote in her journal, "Last year I had no support system or extra help in coping with the immense problems and little everyday things that happen. I felt alone. I learned to cope by myself. I worked 14 hours a day. This year . . . I have a network of people to call on for help or ideas. I can hardly believe what a positive influence the communication has had on my life. I don't have to reinvent the wheel anymore." Participants asked to assess their experiences with the project especially and repeatedly lauded the mentoring support they received (Jonson, 1998, pp. 23-24).

Each of the preceding examples has similarities with the others; these and other programs also have many characteristics that vary. Most, for example, are set up with one-on-one relationships between a mentor and a mentee. In some programs, however, individuals—including a mentor, sometimes several mentees, and other school representatives—collaborate to provide resources and support for the beginning teachers. In some, as in Kentucky, mentors are paid for a fixed amount of time. In others, a stipend—or other type of benefit—is provided, and the mentor and mentee determine their own schedule. In a few programs, such as in Minneapolis, the mentorship is a full-time job conducted during a temporary leave from standard teaching responsibilities.

Despite their differences, successful mentoring programs have certain things in common. Seven elements of a strong program are listed in Box 2.1.

Box 2.1

Elements of a Strong Mentoring Program

1. Mentors are selected based on specific qualifications, including but not limited to teaching ability. Listening skills and the ability to empathize with new teachers are only two of the many other necessary qualifications.

2. Mentors are provided with specific training for their role.

3. Mentors continue to receive support throughout the process, just as they give support to their mentees.

4. Mentors are paired with mentees based on criteria established within the program.

5. Mentors establish relationships with their mentees based on trust and respect.

6. Mentors receive some form of recognition for their work.

7. The mentoring program is evaluated and refined on an ongoing basis.

QUALIFICATIONS OF A GOOD MENTOR

Good teachers of children are not necessarily good teachers of adults. Although the obvious qualifications of skill in teaching and command of the curriculum are essential for a good mentor, they alone are not enough. The good mentor must also have a thorough understanding of both state and national standards. In addition, he or she must be sensitive to the needs of the beginning teacher, be able to transmit effective teaching strategies, be a good listener, be able to communicate openly with the beginning teacher, understand that teachers may be effective using a variety of styles, refrain from being judgmental, and model the philosophy that education is an ongoing process. Desirable personality traits include wisdom, caring, humor, and nurturing. Commitment to the profession is also essential.

In a survey of teacher-mentors within the San Francisco Unified School District (Jonson, 1999b), only 6 of 28 respondents mentioned professional teaching skills when asked what they considered to be the most important qualities in a good mentor. Nearly half mentioned "listening," with other frequently listed attributes including "supportive," "nonjudgmental," "positive," and "having a good sense of humor." One respondent summarized particularly well what most seemed to say: "I think what [the mentees] valued most was emotional support—though of course practical ideas are good—[also] sensitivity [and] knowledge of subject matter and methodologies."

Understanding of Standards. During the past 10 years, educators have struggled with establishing standards and with the challenges associated with standardized assessments. Many have expressed concerns about overemphasizing testing and about misused tests. Even so, beginning teachers need to approach standards with a clear focus. They need to start from the pragmatic premise of the promise of standards.

Matt Gandal and Jennifer Vranek (2001) of Project Achieve, a bipartisan group created by U.S. governors and business leaders, argue that teaching a common body of essential skills and knowledge does not narrow the curriculum or inhibit good teaching practice. The more we expect from students, the more they will achieve, Gandal and Vranek note. From their examination of state and national policies, they have formulated what is needed for standards to have an impact: "teachable, parsimonious standards"; rich and rigorous tests that align with the standards; assistance and professional supports for teachers; and "a fighting chance for students"—extra help, more time, resources, whatever it takes to boost achievement (pp. 6-13).

Mentors can assist beginning teachers to understand that high and rigorous academic standards are

- A way to establish what all students need to know and be able to do
- A result of a public and political outcry for increased accountability in schools
- Not yet well implemented in most schools, although not for lack of trying
- Fraught with challenges and difficulties but still an opportunity to raise the achievement of all
- A bipartisan reform that offers a common ground on which all advocates of good education can unite (Scherer, 2001, p. 5)

Sensitivity to the Needs of the Beginning Teacher. Understanding the needs of the beginning teacher is at the core of being an effective mentor. The mentor must be empathetic with the beginner and keep in mind that the mentee is still developing, both personally and professionally. Most experienced teachers remember those first years and the stresses of being new to the profession (see Chapter 3). Only those who can understand and empathize with the problems and concerns of the beginner—and who can keep in mind the basic skills required of all teachers (see Chapter 4)—are truly able to support the protégé, offer constructive assistance, and reduce rather than add to the beginning teacher's feeling of being overwhelmed. One of the San Francisco mentors surveyed noted as one of the most important qualifications for good mentoring simply "remembering my first year—with no one to help me along" (Jonson, 1999b).

Ability to Transmit Effective Teaching Strategies. No matter how successful a teacher is in reaching young children, she will not make a good mentor unless she can also convey those strategies to the adult learner. Techniques for doing this include providing direct assistance, demonstration teaching, observing the mentee and providing feedback, role modeling, reflecting with the mentee, and discussing formally in conferences or informally at other times in ways that are meaningful to another adult (see Chapters 5 and 6). As one San Francisco respondent noted, a good mentor is able to give "a wealth of practical strategies from which [mentees] can build their own system" (Jonson, 1999b).

Ability to Listen. Of the 28 San Francisco mentors who responded to a question about what they considered to be the most important qualifications for serving as a mentor, nearly half mentioned "listening" at or near the top of their lists. In fact, listening was the most frequently noted individual characteristic. In several cases, the respondent further pointed out that a mentor must have *time* to listen. Others coupled listening with giving support and encouragement.

All too often, the beginning teacher simply needs to talk to someone about what has happened during the day. Although this may not seem to be a difficult need to fill, working alone in the classroom does not leave open any possibility of discussing ideas during the routine workday. Sometimes the act of sitting by while the beginning teacher talks can itself help a protégé to reflect on a situation and figure out what went well, what did not, and how things could have been different. At other times, the mentor might help further by asking questions that then guide the beginning teacher to his own solutions, or the mentor might provide support simply by confirming a mentee's thoughts or letting him know that his concern is valid or typical.

Ability to Communicate Openly With the Beginning Teacher. Several San Francisco mentors cited communication and openness as being required for good mentoring. Being open means being willing to share experiences and materials with the mentee without reserve. It is part of what makes a mentor-mentee relationship strong. Respondents often followed or preceded the word *open* with *nonjudgmental* or *accessible,* other frequently noted mentor qualities.

According to J. B. Rowley (1999), a professor of education who has spent the past decade helping to establish mentor programs, a primary requirement for good mentoring is the ability to communicate hope and optimism. He writes,

> Good mentor-teachers capitalize on opportunities to affirm the human potential of their mentees. They do so in private conversations and in public settings. Good mentors share their own struggles and frustrations and how they overcame them. And always, they do so in a genuine and caring way that engenders trust. (Rowley, 1999, p. 22)

Understanding of Diverse Teaching Styles. It is important that a mentor have "the ability to recognize and nurture a beginning teacher in finding his own style, strengths, and weaknesses," according to one San Francisco mentor. Another mentor noted the importance of allowing the beginning teacher "space to discover her own teaching style while being close by in case the mentor is needed" (Jonson, 1999b). This same mentor felt it was important not to interfere with the instructional strategies established by the beginning teacher.

Each of these experienced mentors recognized the importance of providing support and assistance without attempting to impose an individual style on the beginning teacher. Only with such an understanding will the beginning teacher have the opportunity to grow in his own personal way.

Restraint From Judgment. Experienced mentors agree that being nonjudgmental is key to the success of a mentor program. Only if a beginning teacher believes she is not being judged will she be willing to share ideas, take risks, and develop her skills to the fullest. A mentee who feels that she is being judged or criticized is more likely to work with and talk about teaching techniques and processes that are comfortable, those that she feels she has already mastered to some extent. She is likely to feel vulnerable when discussing problems or concerns—which defeats the point of having a mentor in the first place.

If the mentor is nonjudgmental, on the other hand, the beginning teacher is more likely to admit difficulties and seek out the help supposed to be provided in the mentor-mentee relationship. The beginning teacher is also more likely to experiment with new, more creative teaching techniques when in the presence of the mentor.

Along with being nonjudgmental, most—but not all—experienced mentors believe that mentors should not be involved in evaluation of the mentee in any way. Again, beginning teachers feel less vulnerable discussing problems and concerns with someone who will not later evaluate them. In many programs, in fact, confidentiality is considered essential and helps bring about trust between the mentor and the mentee.

In a few programs, like the one in Minneapolis, the mentor does play some role in evaluating the beginning teacher. The idea there is that the mentor knows the beginning teacher better than most other potential evaluators and that an assessment from a mentor is fairer than one from another evaluator might be. In the Minneapolis program, evaluation that might affect retention occurs only after the beginning teacher's third year in the profession.

The California Formative Assessment and Support System for Teachers (CFASST), a massive state-supported reform effort begun in 1999 to improve teaching, also involves assessment—but not for the purposes of retention decisions. At the core of the CFASST program are mentoring relationships, new teaching standards, and *formative* assessment tools—that is, assessment intended to help teachers improve practice, not to be used as a basis for formal teacher evaluation. CFASST requires that these assessments be implemented within the context of local programs to support beginning teachers. In this "nonjudgmental" mode, mentors and novice teachers reflect together on teaching in relation to student learning. Rather than evaluate the beginning teacher's effectiveness through cursory administrative observations and judgments, CFASST puts veteran and beginning teachers together to constantly grapple with how best to address the varied academic, social, and emotional needs of their students.

Without a strong relationship built on common experience, trust, and a nonjudgmental stance, a mentoring program is not likely to succeed. In one California system, for example, coaches are hired to work with 15 to 18 new teachers at various schools throughout the district. "I was assigned a PAR [Peer Assistance Review] coach, who was not a peer because she doesn't teach elementary school, not an assistant because she never once offered to help in any way, and not a coach because she never modeled a single lesson plan for me or any of her first-year teachers at [my school]," said one discouraged beginning teacher (quoted in Harrington, 2001, p. 1). She and other beginning teachers in the PAR program have said that the coach seemed more like a judge than a mentor. After less than eight hours of observing the beginning teacher, the coach wrote an evaluation. The beginning teacher felt that the coach spent the year judging and criticizing her, despite the fact that the coach worked at a middle school (unlike the elementary school where the beginning teacher worked) and with a very different student population than the largely Hispanic and socioeconomically disadvantaged population at the elementary school (Harrington, 2001, p. 1).

Modeling of Continuous Learning. One of the key ideas behind any mentor-mentee program is that learning is a continuous process, not a finite experience that ends with the receipt of a diploma upon graduation from an accredited teacher education program. Mentoring is one way to provide the beginning teacher with continuing education specific to his situation. It is crucial that the mentor model for the new teacher the importance of continuing education by partaking in further learning herself.

Being a mentor is in itself a means for continuing to learn. The mentor-teacher can get new ideas from the novice teacher—just as Nancy learned a new attention-getting technique from Dolores—and should not be afraid to let the beginning teacher know this. In addition, the mentor can (a) attend workshops, conferences, and graduate classes, sometimes with the mentee, sometimes with the aid of mentor program funding designated for such career development; (b) experiment with new methods, sometimes inspired by the mentee; and (c) write and read articles, sometimes in response to issues that arise within the mentor-mentee relationship.

The mentor should admit to the beginning teacher that he does not have the answers to every question and problem that arises. The mentor, like the mentee, can always learn from others and should be comfortable sharing questions with the mentee. The admission that the mentor, too, is still learning can be encouraging to the beginning teacher, who may be relieved to find that she is not the only person without all the answers. This in itself can be reassuring to a struggling beginner.

EFFECTIVE TRAINING

In February 1997, the U.S. Department of Education's National Center for Education Statistics published its report *Teacher Professionalization and Teacher Commitment: A Multilevel Analysis.* According to that report, having a mentor program to assist beginning teachers is less important than the quality of that assistance for improving teacher performance and commitment (Portner, 1998, p. 4). In other words, a mentor program is much more helpful if it's well thought out. A formal, high-quality program is significantly more likely to be effective than a program in which the mentor is simply assigned to a mentee and then set loose.

Mentoring requires commitment to the program, and this is sometimes best attained when the mentor has a clear definition of the roles and responsibilities required. In effective programs, mentors receive at the outset a specific description of these roles and responsibilities. They may receive relevant reading materials to get them started as well. They also receive some level of formal training.

Training might be conducted by a program coordinator (a sort of "mentors' mentor") or by a school administrator. This leader sets up conferences and workshops to discuss techniques, goals, skills, and attitudes. Although some of this training should happen before work actually begins with the beginning teachers, training should continue after mentors have formed a working relationship with their mentees.

MENTOR SUPPORT

To have a successful program, according to five mentors in Marin County, California, support providers should meet regularly with each other to discuss successes and questions and to talk about teaching (Smith, 1993, p. 15). Three of the five mentors did not feel they had been supported in their role and named this lack of support as their chief concern and source of anxiety about the program (Smith, 1993, p. 14).

Like the beginning teacher (and even the experienced teacher), the beginning mentor (and even the experienced mentor) needs to discuss issues. Support must be ongoing and readily available. In some districts, mentors may meet in support groups to discuss problems and questions. A program coordinator or other administrator should also be available to discuss issues as needed and to help locate resources for the mentor, both generally and when specifically requested. In some districts, an experienced mentor may observe a beginning mentor in action, just as the beginning mentor (experienced teacher) observes a beginning teacher in action. Finally, some districts publish a mentor newsletter dealing with issues of concern to the readership (Smith, 1993, p. 15). The newsletter could also commend the work of mentors and beginning teachers as a reward for good work and a source of ideas for others.

In addition to emotional and educational support, more practical types of support are also necessary for a program to work effectively. Most important, *time* must be provided for this important duty. This could be in the form of a substitute teacher releasing the mentor from the classroom to be with the beginning teacher, or it could mean release time from non-teaching responsibilities, such as playground or hall duty. A program can also be strengthened significantly by funding for workshops and training, both in the field of mentoring itself and in areas relevant for the beginning teacher.

MENTOR-TO-MENTEE PAIRING

Matches between mentors and mentees are sometimes based on convenience and availability. In a small program, in fact, there may be little choice of mentors for a beginning teacher. Ideally, though, criteria should be established for pairing the beginning teacher with a mentor who will serve as the richest learning resource available. These criteria might include the following:

- Proximity

- Same or close grade level

- Same or related subject area

- Common lunch or planning period

- Similar personality or educational philosophy

Experts disagree regarding this last item. Some believe that a mentor who understands and believes in the beginning teacher's philosophies and styles will be better able to help and that the relationship will be more comfortable with shared beliefs. Others say that two teachers will learn more from each other if they have different styles (ASCD, 1999a, p. 109).

According to the San Francisco mentors surveyed (Jonson 1999b), proximity is a particularly relevant issue for effectiveness of the pairing. Of 27 mentors who responded to a question about whether their mentees were likely to come to them or to someone else for assistance, 24 said their mentees came to them in at least some cases. The three who did not get questions from their mentees all cited location as the problem: Beginning teachers were more likely to go first to someone nearby, they said. One other respondent said that of four mentees, two were on-site and came first to the mentor; the other two were at different sites and talked to someone else first.

Even of those who said their mentees *were* likely to come to them, one qualified the response by explaining, "Mentees need instantaneous assistance sometimes and will first seek help at their own school site. If the problem doesn't need immediate solution—they then seek help from me." Another wrote, "For resources . . . and also for class management/discipline [the mentee comes to me]. It is more convenient for the mentee to confer with site staff for logistics." Yet another wrote, "It depends on the issue. It is very common for teachers to go to the *closest* teacher (i.e., next door) for simple questions. I think my mentees seek me out for more challenging issues" (Jonson, 1999b).

All in all, 10 respondents mentioned proximity as an issue in how frequently the mentee consulted the mentor for advice. One even mentioned that having different lunch periods was a problem. Four said that teaching at different grade levels prevented them from working together on all issues. Teachers working in different-level schools are even less likely to have a successful relationship. Kindergarten, first-grade, and even fifth-grade teachers, for example, face very different challenges than do single-subject teachers of teenagers at high schools.

Mentor-mentee matches are often made by a principal and other committee members who have interviewed the teachers involved. A program coordinator who has worked with the mentor also often has insights regarding appropriate pairings. Pairings are made very early in a beginning teacher's career, however, often before that teacher's needs and strengths are realized. Occasionally, even with strong mentors, the match does not serve the needs of the beginning teacher as expected. If this happens, a good system should have built into it some way for a new pairing to be made without any blame placed (ASCD, 1999a, p. 110). Program coordinators should never lose sight of the focus: to provide the beginning teacher with the most help possible to enable her to make a transition to the professional world during her first years on the job.

ESTABLISHMENT OF THE MENTOR-MENTEE RELATIONSHIP

For a mentor-mentee relationship to be most effective, the beginning teacher and the mentor must get along both personally and professionally. According to research, the success of a relationship is generally based on two things: (a) whether the protégé respects the mentor as a person and (b) whether the protégé admires the mentor's knowledge, experience, and style (Jonson, 1997, p. 9).

If the beginning teacher is assigned to a mentor who is critical, excessively task oriented, uncaring, and unpredictable, that new teacher will be concerned primarily with gaining the favor of the mentor and avoiding criticism. If, on the other hand, the mentor has developed a trusting relationship with the beginning teacher—one in which the mentor has proven to be safe, predictable, and supportive—the protégé is more likely to take risks, to try new ideas, and to develop new skills with the mentor's aid (ASCD, 1999a, p. 95). In the example at the beginning of this chapter,

Dolores and Nancy seem to have a compatible and collegial relationship. It is this type of trusting, positive, productive relationship that every mentor needs to strive for from the very beginning of a relationship.

In fact, *trust* was the most common word used by San Francisco mentors to explain why they thought their mentees came to them for assistance. Other things considered important for a successful mentor-mentee relationship were having an outgoing personality, being cheerful and helpful, being willing to let mentees try their own solutions, and letting the mentee know that any communications would be confidential. Box 2.2 offers some tips for establishing a good relationship with a mentee.

Although experts seem to agree universally that the nature of the relationship is key to the success of the mentoring program, creating the required trust in the beginning, when time to socialize is limited, can be difficult. How does one get to know a beginning teacher at the start of a year, when so many tasks are required—from setting up the room to getting to know the children to finalizing or adjusting curriculum?

Some suggestions for building a relationship with a beginning teacher early in the year include eating lunch together, taking a trip to a teacher supply store, sharing family pictures, bringing the beginning teacher a cup of coffee in the morning or a soda after school and sitting to have a chat, touring the school together, or taking a drive around the school neighborhood. The ASCD (1999a, p. 92) also suggests the following tips for mentors wanting to get a relationship off to a good start:

1. Prepare your classroom early to leave time available when the beginning teacher needs help.

2. While working with the beginning teacher to set up his room, use the time to talk and identify his biggest short-term concerns. Set up times to work together to accomplish these tasks. This effort will demonstrate to the beginning teacher that you will be there at "crunch time."

3. While cutting out letters for bulletin boards or arranging desks, talk about each other's family, background, and teaching dreams. This will reduce the beginning teacher's stress, help begin to build a relationship, and allow you to address some critical needs.

In addition to getting to know the beginning teacher in general, the mentor should try to learn something about the mentee's expectations of the program. Some beginning teachers—like some students—are hungry to learn, eager for advice. Others are defensive at first (Rowley, 1999, p. 21), resistant to assistance. Regardless of personality, the mentor must work with the beginning teacher, adapting to the style and needs of the individual. Box 2.3 lists some questions a mentor can ask of a mentee.

Box 2.2

Tips for Establishing a Strong Mentor-Mentee Relationship

The following advice is based on responses from San Francisco mentors to a question asking how they built trusting relationships with their mentees:

- Have regular contact, both formal and informal. Let the mentee know that you are there for her.
- Build trust on respect, open communication, and support. Attempt to offer as much of these as possible.
- Make regular phone calls. Share unit plans and resources.
- Let him know that he can be open and honest with his needs. He does not need to fear judgment.
- Have informal visits and conversations. Socialize. Be available in a timely manner.
- Try to be nonjudgmental and open. Never talk about a new teacher behind her back.
- Listen. Respond to his questions. Provide a variety of resources.
- Validate the challenges of teaching. Take her ideas and feelings seriously. Help her to trust her own judgment.
- Discuss problems realistically and let him know that you have the same problems sometimes. Let him vent.
- Hold meetings for new teachers at the school. Focus in part on school activities, but mostly allow the meetings to be open-ended so the teachers can bring concerns and questions as well as stories of success.
- Offer support. Be positive. Ask what she needs.
- Talk with mentees. Share materials and resources. Get together with them socially. Take an active interest in their classrooms.
- Tell the mentee at the first meeting that whatever is said goes no further. Be warm and caring. Share your own experiences as a teacher—good and bad.
- Be accessible. Be willing to diverge and help in areas the mentee feels are more pressing.
- Treat him as a young peer. Confide in him. Talk frankly, openly, and honestly.
- Show that it is a mutually beneficial relationship—she benefits from your experience, and you benefit from her exuberance and technical skills.
- Observe together. Talk about areas other than teaching. Joke. Let the mentee know your strengths and weaknesses.
- Be available, open, and honest. Be reliable, and follow through with activities.

Box 2.3

Questions a Mentor Might Want Answered Early On

1. What does the beginning teacher value in teaching?

2. Why is the beginning teacher working with a mentor? Did she request a mentor, or was the relationship mandatory?

3. How much does the beginning teacher know about the subject she is teaching? Is it her primary subject, or was she assigned to teach something she's not comfortable with?

4. What is her teaching background?

5. What structures has she put in place for classroom management?

6. How is she as a learner? Is she comfortable with new ideas? What is she ready to try?

SOURCE: Fraser (1998, p. 9).

RECOGNITION OF SERVICE

For any program to be successful, the participants need to feel recognized and valued. Chapter 7 discusses in more detail the many benefits of serving as a mentor, but it is important to note here that although some of the biggest benefits are in personal and professional growth and self-satisfaction for the mentor, a good program should have built into it more tangible rewards as well (see Box 2.4).

Whatever the specific program, no system should take for granted the time and contribution of a good mentor. The mentor's enthusiasm and contribution to the school must be recognized if the program is to be successful, just as the beginning teacher must feel appreciated if he is to continue in his role. Continuity will keep the program strong and ensure the growth that comes with experience.

PROGRAM EVALUATION

Mentoring programs are only one of many strategies used for professional development. Just as with other strategies, evaluation needs to be built into these programs from their inception, and evidence must be gathered throughout the process to determine their effectiveness (Guskey, 2000). In the first year of a new program, evaluators should assess the operation of the program: Is implementation occurring as expected? How could it be

---

Box 2.4

Possible Rewards to Recognize Mentor Service

- Reduced class size
- Opportunity to team teach with a protégé
- Release from other duties (e.g., hall or yard duty)
- Paid attendance at conferences or workshops
- Graduate school tuition
- An end-of-year recognition banquet or luncheon
- A formal recognition ceremony before the board of education or school faculty
- A stipend

---

improved? Over the next few years, focus should move to achievement of goals and purposes: Is the retention rate for beginning teachers improving? Are both beginning and experienced teachers gaining new knowledge, skills, and strategies? Are collegiality and collaboration among faculty increasing? Are students learning more (Portner, 2001, p. 84)?

Structured interviews, observations, and surveys are all good techniques for gathering information to be used for program evaluation. Other sources of information might include teachers' journal entries, informal or formal discussions, and questionnaires administered to both mentors and mentees (Portner, 2001, p. 92). The information gathered can then be used as a basis for improving the program through constant fine-tuning and modification. In addition, this information is important for accountability purposes and should affect decisions regarding continuation of the program (p. 89).

CONCLUSION

In the scenario at the beginning of this chapter, Nancy was able to help Dolores see her own strengths and to offer suggestions for furthering Dolores's development as a beginning teacher. The Virginia program in which these two teachers participated was well structured, and the pairing between the teachers was good.

Although individual programs throughout the country vary, all successful ones include some common elements. This chapter looked at seven key elements for effective mentoring programs. One of those elements was that mentors are selected based on specific qualifications, including the ability to empathize with beginning teachers. Chapter 3 serves to remind the experienced teacher of the many stresses common for teaching professionals as they begin their new careers. It is certain to increase the mentor's empathy as she works with the beginning teacher.

The mentor relationship is one of the most developmentally important relationships a person can have in early adulthood.

—Daniel Levinson, *Seasons of a Man's Life* (1986)

3

Remembering
the First Days

A s a newly hired teacher, I recall being shown to my classroom just
prior to the beginning of school. There were four blank walls, some
boxes of crayons, rulers, paper, and a few textbooks in the room. After
unlocking the door, the smiling secretary waved good-bye and wished me
good luck! A thick lump formed at the back of my throat and started
spreading downward. I was totally alone and, although I was trained in a
fine university program, the enormity of organizing the bits and pieces
into a learning environment eluded me. The thought of being responsible
for thirty small children for the next nine months nearly panicked me.

—Leila Christenbury (1995, p. 3)

To understand the role of the mentor in education, it is helpful for mentors to think back to some of their own first-year teaching experiences and
the anxieties they felt. The fears of the teacher quoted here are common to
many novices to the profession, and most veterans will probably remember similar experiences if they try. Before meeting with the beginning
teacher, a mentor should try to recall: What was that first year like? What
caused anxiety? What unexpected problems arose? How were they
resolved? Did any particular individual help out? If so, was the individ-

ual assigned to help, or did a sympathetic colleague simply take the initiative to become involved? How did it feel to be new to the job? How would it have been if no one had stepped in? Or, if no one did step in, how could things have been different if someone had?

Entering the teaching profession presents challenges not experienced in any other field. Only a teacher would carry the same load in the first year as an experienced colleague carries—sometimes under even more difficult circumstances. Only a teacher would work completely isolated from other professionals, responsible for a roomful of children, with students and parents alike expecting the same proficiency as from the 20-year veteran.

Researchers Brown and Williams (1977), Ryan (1986), and Bush (1996), have outlined the following characteristics typical of the first year in the teaching profession:

- A beginning teacher's job description is essentially the same as the teacher's down the hall who has 5, 10, or even 15 years of experience.
- Teaching is generally done in isolation. The system does not encourage observation of others' teaching, the sharing of ideas, or group lesson planning.
- Beginning teachers often get the most-difficult-to-teach students and other "hand-me-downs" of the system: old textbooks, desks, and schedules.
- Teaching must be experienced in order to be clearly understood. Sitting at a student's desk for 16 years does not give a true picture of what teaching is really like.
- Student teaching experiences, in general, are not extensive enough to provide a teacher with the full breadth of experiences necessary to be a master teacher.

All too often, beginning teachers find themselves doing the jobs that others have discarded. They end up teaching the class sections nobody else wants; rotated into certain duties that others know enough to avoid; and given the least attractive, most awkwardly appointed classrooms (Moran, 1990, p. 213). Middle and high school teachers may end up teaching classes in a variety of subject areas, regardless of the teacher's area of focus. One new middle school teacher, for instance, found herself planning for two math, one social science, and two physical education classes.

Given these circumstances, no matter how thorough the beginning teacher's preparation has been—no matter how "ready" that teacher feels on the first day of school—it probably isn't enough. Figure 3.1 shows just some of the problems beginning teachers are likely to face. Yet despite the confusion so soon encountered, beginning teachers are often reluctant to ask colleagues for help because they fear that they might be considered incompetent. They might refrain from asking principals for advice because they worry that exposing their difficulties could lead to a negative evaluation. "It is professional suicide to admit you need help," one beginning teacher said (Pearson & Honig, 1992, p. 5). "You learn this fast so you don't go up to your department chair or other teachers for help."

Figure 3.1. Problems Confronting New Teachers

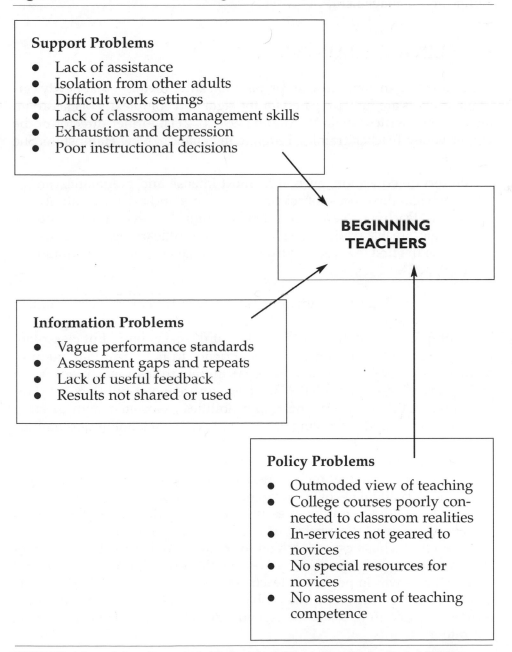

SOURCE: Adapted from Pearson & Honig, *The California New Teacher Project* (1992).

Even if a beginning teacher does want to consult professionally with an experienced colleague, a busy day may not allow it; struggling onward might seem to be a better use of time. All too often, without an effective induction program, the beginning teacher muddles through, sometimes surviving, sometimes leaving the profession in frustration. Without communicating with other teachers, the beginning teacher may not realize that these frustrations are typical, that others have the same problems with discipline and management.

PRESERVICE TRAINING

"The oldest myth about teacher preparation still prevails—that newly certified teachers are fully prepared for the rigor and complexity of classroom instruction," writes Sheila W. Moran (1990, p. 211), former director of the Upper Valley Teacher Training Program in Lebanon, New Hampshire. She continues,

> Preservice education, even at its most intense and pragmatic, can only begin the process of scientific discovery and artistic creativity that is teaching. Newly certified teachers, however bright and capable, are just ready to begin the meaningful learning that occurs during the first few years of true professional engagement. (Moran 1990, p. 211)

Bartell (1995, p. 28) points out that university coursework builds a teacher's conceptual understanding, and clinical or field experience helps prepare the teacher for the reality of the classroom. But classroom knowledge itself comes only from experience in the classroom environment (Doyle, 1990). "No matter what initial professional preparation they receive," writes Bartell (1995), "teachers are never fully prepared for classroom realities and for the responsibilities associated with meeting the needs of a rapidly growing, increasingly diverse student population" (p. 29).

A significant majority of the new teachers surveyed for a Public Agenda report noted that their preservice training had included "too little about the nuts and bolts of teaching: how to run classrooms, maintain discipline, deal with the routine pressures of their profession and even how to teach effectively" (Raspberry, 2000, p. 3). None of the teachers surveyed had been in the business of teaching for more than 5 years. In contrast, of 900 education professors interviewed in the same study, 37% did not believe that it was important to teach teachers how to maintain discipline and order in the classroom. The problem is not a lack of concern from the professors, according to Public Agenda President Deborah Wadsworth, but rather that they have a very different mind-set. They . . . seem to assume a sort of glorified environment in which every youngster comes to school problem-free and eager. . . . They are almost tone-deaf to the things the young classroom teachers are telling us they need. (Raspberry, 2000, p. 3)

The California Commission on the Teaching Profession reports that the coursework required for a teaching credential is poorly connected both to current theory about how to teach and to the reality of teaching in a classroom. In addition, "the teacher's workplace is organized and supervised in ways that isolate and hobble teachers," it states. "Qualities that are seen as hallmarks of productivity in business—mutual help, exchange of ideas, cooperative work to develop better practices—are rare in schools" (Pearson & Honig, 1992, p. 11).

In a San Diego County study, all of 15 new middle and high school teachers interviewed noted that the actual practice of teaching was often inconsistent with the theory they had learned in their coursework. "Student teaching and actual teaching are such completely different experiences," one explained. "When I was student teaching, someone was always there for me if I needed them. Now, I'm expected to know everything and do everything right and I know I'm not doing it right. I feel like the rope got cut and I'm floating. Actually, sometimes I feel like I'm falling" (Mathison, 1996, p. 16).

Rarely do teachers anticipate this extreme gulf between their training and reality. Most begin their first assignments feeling prepared and having high expectations for themselves and their students. Given the stress of their first year, though, they often lose confidence in themselves and their abilities when they find that their preparation has not been adequate.

THE NEED FOR WARM BODIES

The problems of beginning teachers are exacerbated for those who lack preservice preparation altogether. A growing number of beginning teachers are coming to the classroom without the preservice training that leads to a teaching credential. In Los Angeles, for example, more than half of the new teachers hired for the 2000-2001 school year lacked a certificate. About one fourth of the district's teachers went to work with only emergency credentials; these teachers were concentrated in schools with the most disadvantaged students (Gursky, 2000). In places like Los Angeles, the shortage of teachers has reached epic proportions. "The problem is getting worse, not better," says Doug Scott, spokesperson for the California Department of Education. "This is not a shortage. This is a crisis. We are literally attacking it as if we were in round-the-clock combat" (Gursky, 2000, p. 11).

The future is likely to bring more such problems. As school enrollments grow and as more teachers retire, the nation faces a huge challenge in training, hiring, and retaining enough teachers. California needs to hire 300,000 new teachers during the next decade. Nationwide, an estimated 2 million teachers will be needed to staff our schools in the next 10 years. Furthermore, the move to reduce class sizes in many states and districts has increased the demand for teachers. California, with its high-profile statewide class-reduction initiative, is a textbook example. Class-size reduction has caused districts to hire huge numbers of uncertified teachers, which threatens to dilute the positive impact of smaller classes.

Commentators such as Arthur Levine, president of Teacher's College, warn that the increasing need for teachers is colliding with simultaneous efforts to toughen hiring requirements (Levine, 1999). Too many classrooms end up being staffed with teachers who are working with emergency or provisional certificates. In a nationwide study by Public Agenda, most school administrators reported facing at least some type of teacher shortage, and two thirds (66%) said they have had to go through extra effort in recent years to recruit the teachers they need. Nationwide, urban educators report feeling the crunch more than educators in suburban districts. More than twice as many urban educators (26% urban, compared with 11% suburban) said they are feeling a critical, widespread shortage, and a large majority (78%) said they have had to go through extra recruiting efforts (Farkas et al., 2000).

Mentoring for beginning teachers often takes place within the context of this need for "warm bodies" to staff classrooms. Many of those working with emergency or provisional certificates especially require assistance as they jump unprepared into the profession. Even more so than fully trained teachers, these emergency teachers are in danger of becoming overwhelmed and discouraged without the help of an experienced colleague.

REALITY SHOCK

Literature on beginning teachers has outlined the stages of teacher development (Moir, 1999), beginning with the induction stage, or the first few years of teaching. This stage has been identified as a unique and important time in a teacher's career. During the induction period, first-year teachers generally experience what Ryan (1986) labeled *reality shock:* the transition from being a student who learns about teaching to actually being a teacher. Reality shock may be experienced in a variety of ways and to different degrees, depending on the individual. Preparation, familiarity with the setting of the first job, and difficulty of the teaching assignment may all affect the degree of shock.

Studies of beginning-teacher development continue to document that the early years of teaching are difficult and stressful and fail to provide for careful, thoughtful development of teaching expertise (Bullough, 1990; Darling-Hammond, 1988; Huling-Austin, 1987, 1992). Most beginning teachers experience daily classroom responsibility as a baptism by fire; many, over the course of their first year, lose faith in their own efficacy and in the learning potential of their students. Beginning teachers typically report worrying about "their kids" every waking hour and may even dream about them. "I feel overwhelmed," one beginning teacher wrote in a journal. "I knew teaching was a tough job, but nothing could have prepared me for all these problems and pitfalls."

It is easy to document that teachers' work environments are less than optimal, contributing to beginning-teacher "reality shock." Mentors—as well as superintendents and site administrators—need to think carefully about five workplace factors inherent in the professional lives of beginning teachers: the legacy of the one-room schoolhouse, inverse beginner responsibilities, restricted choices, invisibility and isolation, and lack of professional dialogue.

The Legacy of the One-Room Schoolhouse. The vestige of pioneer times—when most schools had one teacher, one group of students, within one confined area—is still evident in most schools today. In many cases, the one-room schoolhouse is repeated every few yards down the school corridor. In these schools, so-called egg-carton schools, each teacher works within her own separate, insulated hole. Many teachers believe, "This is *my* classroom, *my* professional world; these are *my* students, *my* materials—and others should leave me alone." In contrast, recent school reform movements have demonstrated that teachers in successful schools are more likely to speak of "*our* students, *our* materials, *our* goals, and what *we* are trying to do." Beginning teachers are more likely to prosper in open, collaborative environments such as these.

Inverse Beginner Responsibilities. Too often, experienced teachers protect their own turf and pass the leftovers on to new teachers. Often when a teacher resigns or retires, the teachers remaining in the school descend upon the classroom to remove materials, equipment, and furniture of value and replace it with their own discards. The new teacher enters a classroom equipped with what no one else wanted. This situation extends even to students themselves; some administrators, faced with a vocal and demanding tenured staff, end up assigning the most difficult and lowest-achieving students to the beginning teacher. All in all, beginning teachers are often left with the most demanding students and with picked-over classrooms. The message to beginning teachers is, "Welcome to teaching. Let's see if you can make it."

Restricted Choices. In many states and school districts, the working lives of teachers are too often bureaucratic and restricted. Teachers have few choices. Their schedules are set, and beginning teachers especially are told what, when, and how to teach. Their input is not solicited. With the current nationwide movement toward standards and testing—minimum competencies, mandated curriculum, and externally developed policies— teachers' professional lives are filled with even more mandates and less choice. Goodlad (1984) reported in his classic nationwide study *A Place Called School* that teachers had virtually no involvement in schoolwide decisions.

Invisibility and Isolation. Glickman (1985) reported that only some 50% of all experienced teachers have ever been observed for purposes of instructional improvement, and only 24% have been observed by another teacher in their school. This pattern changed somewhat in the 1980s and 1990s, when principals were encouraged to be "instructional leaders." This paradigm is now being challenged, however, as teachers question how appropriate it is for principals to serve dual roles, supervising teachers in a management capacity (e.g., evaluating their performance) and also trying to help them improve instruction.

Lack of Professional Dialogue. Because most classrooms are closed off from one another, teachers rarely talk together as professionals. Researchers have reported that professional talk among teachers lasts less than two minutes per day (Glickman, 1985). Teachers spend an overwhelming amount of their time talking to students and socializing with each other but little time solving instructional problems together.

In attempting to struggle through these inherent blocks to teacher development in their work environments, conscientious beginning teachers may become consumed by the daily responsibilities of teaching. "When I first started teaching high school English, I was not very good at it," one beginning teacher recalls,

> and I knew it. I hoped, though, that no one else would find out before I had a chance to fix things, and so I kept my door to my classroom firmly shut. I didn't want other teachers in my room; I didn't want administrators or parents. Because I knew I was stumbling and lurching through my lesson plans, I didn't even want to talk about what I was doing—or thinking of doing—in my classroom. (Christenbury, 1995, p. 3)

FEARS AND ANXIETIES OF BEGINNING TEACHERS

Many veteran teachers have vivid memories of their first-year teaching experiences, some of them intensely emotional. The often-voiced contention that the first year is one of trauma, drama, and basic survival may be overstated, but all beginning teachers do have special needs, problems, and concerns.

"The first months and years of teaching are full of pain, confusion, loneliness, and often humiliation," writes Moran (1990, p. 211). In thinking back, most teachers will recall particular frustrations with classroom management and discipline and with time management issues. Researchers have identified a number of other crucial issues as well (see Box 3.1). All these issues create stress for the beginning teacher. If left unchecked, this stress can lead to fatigue, and eventually the teacher may choose to leave the profession. But with the help of a good mentor, the beginning teacher can take hold of these issues, rise to the challenge, and move forward.

Classroom Management and Discipline

One of the biggest sources of teacher anxiety, classroom management is the ongoing task of keeping control in the room. Because teachers cannot anticipate the many behavioral events that will occur in their classroom, the beginning teacher often feels unprepared and out of control when they take place. Beginning teachers may feel incompetent when they don't know how to handle discipline and may experience particular anxiety when they cannot control disruptions. In many studies, teachers have noted specifically that they felt classroom management and discipline procedures should be given much more attention in preparation curriculum (e.g., Mathison, 1996, p. 15).

Teachers have good reason for this concern. In 11 of 15 classrooms observed in the San Diego study of new teachers, researchers found that the general classroom environment was "uncontrolled and chaotic. Students were observed passing notes, holding private conversations, sleeping, and/or generally 'goofing off.'" In a survey of 63 teachers in that same study, 48% said they were often frustrated by the level of talking and

---

Box 3.1

Areas of Particular Concern for Beginning Teachers

- Classroom management and discipline
- Time management
- An overwhelming workload
- Classroom instruction
- Technology in the classroom
- High-stakes accountability
- Sociocultural awareness and sensitivity
- Student motivation
- A solitary work environment
- Relationships with parents and colleagues

general commotion in the classroom, and 24% sometimes felt that they spent most of the class period getting students to settle down (Mathison, 1996, pp. 13-14).

Time Management

First-year teachers are often overwhelmed by the amount of work that needs to be done in a day; in the beginning, they may spend up to 70 hours per week on schoolwork (Moir, 1999). Even within the school day itself, time management can be difficult. Without experience, the beginning teacher may not be able to judge how long an individual lesson or activity will take. If the project takes longer than anticipated, students may not be able to complete it. If it takes less time, the teacher may be left with the problem of unstructured chaos.

Aside from juggling the demands of the job, balancing personal and professional time can be difficult. Complaints from family members and friends, common in the first year, only compound the problems. "I thought I'd be busy, something like student teaching," one new teacher said, "but this is crazy. I'm feeling like I'm constantly running. It's hard to focus on other aspects of my life."

Still others feel as if teaching has completely taken over their lives. One pointed out that teaching is like holding three separate jobs: one during the school day (actually teaching), another in the afternoon after the students leave (attending meetings and dealing with other administrative tasks), and yet a third in the evenings and on weekends (planning and grading papers). Often the beginner finds it impossible to keep school hours within reason and ends up with work encroaching on all aspects of life. "If I only had one day off to plan for every day I teach, I'd be all right," one commented.

An Overwhelming Workload

Under the umbrella of *workload* are not only the activities a teacher must prepare, teaching assignments outside the area of expertise, and assignments to "difficult" classes but also a vast number of extracurricular responsibilities. Beginning teachers often end up with classes larger than those of experienced teachers and, in the upper grades, with a disproportionate number of remedial courses to teach. They may also be assigned to teach a variety of subjects, some of them outside of their primary interest. Extracurricular activities might include committee work, lunch duty, extra counseling, and extracurricular student activities. Paperwork alone can be overwhelming for a teacher who does not have time built into the day to take care of it and who has not anticipated all the forms to come. All in all, the workload of a novice could well be larger—not smaller—than that of a veteran.

Classroom Instruction

In this category are planning and carrying out instruction, as well as locating resources and materials and coping with a wide variety of student abilities in the same class. Using technology effectively and evaluating student progress are two related tasks.

Although all teachers must prepare lesson plans, veteran teachers are at least able to scaffold new concepts, strategies, and curriculum onto their previous learning, knowledge, and experience. Beginning teachers must develop all lessons from the start. Without help, many have difficulty adapting what they have learned in college courses into effective activities for students. In addition, beginning teachers at the middle or high school level often have a wider variety of subject matter to plan for than do those who have been around longer. Teachers in the San Diego study expressed particular frustration at needing to be proficient in different subject areas, sometimes in unrelated disciplines, requiring the development of completely different lesson plans (Mathison, 1996, p. 12). No additional time is provided for this extra workload.

Presenting materials in ways that are both challenging and understandable for students today is difficult. Students entering school now vary widely in their readiness to learn and come with different languages, values, and backgrounds. Working with such a diverse group is especially difficult for teachers who have not been prepared to do so (Pearson & Honig, 1992, p. 11). Assessing these students can also be difficult, again because of the wide variety of backgrounds the children bring with them to school.

Technology in the Classroom

Changes in technology have recently caused additional teacher anxiety. These problems lie both in knowing how to use the equipment with the students and in using the technology effectively for teaching methodology (Wilson, Ireton, & Wood, 1997, p. 400). Only a few years ago, computers in schools were used mainly for enrichment activities and variety or to teach students about computers (i.e., in computer literacy classes)— rarely to provide students with instruction in core academic subjects (Means, 2000, p. 188). Teachers today are expected to engage students in more authentic tasks, however, using tools identical or analogous to those that professionals in the work world employ, such as word processing, databases, and spreadsheets. In some schools, rather than doing math exercises or reading about science topics on a computer, students use computer tools to support their work in complex projects involving math, science, and other subject areas. Many schools have turned to word processing software to support student writing. Teachers worry about the need to keep abreast of all the latest technology. "Everything I know will be obsolete in two years!" laments one.

Teachers also are concerned with equity issues in schools and often feel frustrated by reports that computers are found in four times as many of the nation's wealthiest schools as in the poorest schools (Means, 2000, p. 189). When computers are donated for school use, they may be outdated systems. In one situation, an urban high school was able to obtain 300 new computers for its classrooms—only to find that the computers could not be used because of inadequate electrical infrastructure. Finally, research studies indicate that even when schools serving low-income students do have computers, they tend to use the technology for drill and practice in basic skills rather than more broadly, as tools for learning.

As a twist, recent college graduates who begin teaching careers are often trained in modern computer use; they have learned to use state-of-the-art equipment beyond what the more experienced mentor may be familiar with. Their problem is that they sometimes have difficulty working with the older systems they find in today's schools—without the color printers, high-speed modems, and other peripherals they learned about in their preservice training—and must adjust to the less desirable equipment. In this case, the beginning teacher may well have more training than the mentor does but may need the advice of a mentor for adapting knowledge to available hardware and software. Beginning teachers and their mentors must wrestle with all of these technology issues together.

High-Stakes Accountability

Finally, assessment of students causes tension for many beginning (as well as some experienced) teachers, who wrestle with matching classroom learning objectives to assessments, with the wide variety of assessments, and with assessing standards and benchmarks. Standardized testing can cause anxiety when teachers find themselves being evaluated according to how well their students do. Teachers fear that they will be held personally responsible for students who do not do well even when teachers do not control many of the variables leading to success on standardized tests (Wilson et al., 1997, p. 400).

Complicating matters even more is the fact that teachers and students face overlapping and competing demands from layers of assessments. Most school systems use a variety of large-scale assessments, including district assessments focused on local content standards, state tests reflecting state content standards, norm-referenced tests, and college admission exams. Their interaction greatly compounds the problems in attempting to link classroom and large-scale assessment. The expectation, although not always formally stated, is that all results show steady gains on all measures. Teachers, especially beginning teachers, become confused and frustrated. Where are they supposed to focus their efforts: on district standards or on mandatory, norm-referenced testing? Whose standards are more important: the district's or the state's? What if grade-level texts do not cover what's on the test? In this era of accountability, these are grave concerns in most faculty rooms.

Sociocultural Awareness and Sensitivity

According to the California New Teacher Project (Commission on Teacher Credentialing, 1991), beginning teachers often find themselves assigned to teach in "highly complex environments" that would challenge even a seasoned veteran—for example, in inner-city schools with high percentages of low-income, ethnolinguistically and culturally diverse children. First-year teachers may well deal with ethnic groups with whom they have never had previous contact. Effective teachers celebrate the diversity of cultures in their classrooms and strive to improve human relations among their students. Yet beginning teachers may find it difficult to teach when they don't understand a culture within their classroom and may even fight against a fear of a group they don't understand. Attempting to communicate with parents who do not speak English only adds to the problem.

One beginning high school teacher, for example, spent many hours his first year attempting to convince the parents of several Hispanic students that their children needed to improve their attendance. These students often missed school to help with a younger sibling, to provide transportation for a family member, or, sometimes, to work. The teacher soon became frustrated in his attempts to communicate with the families. He realized that part of the problem was that he did not speak Spanish and needed constantly to rely on translators, often the students themselves. Only after some time did he discover another central problem in communication, however: a difference in values. Although he had seen the problem as a lack of respect for education, he eventually realized that it had more to do with a cultural priority in favor of family. Some of the parents did not understand his concern, he realized, because they felt it was more important for the student to contribute to the family (by caring for a sibling or earning money) than to go to school. A mentor experienced in working with students from this culture might have helped him communicate better and with more understanding from the beginning.

Teachers might also have difficulty working with children who have been abused and may be uncomfortable with the legal requirement that they report a suspicion of abuse. They might work with the children of mothers who abused drugs while pregnant or with children who suffer from autism, processing problems, attention deficit disorder, or attention deficit/hyperactivity disorder, for example. Children growing up in poverty or within transient families may raise unexpected issues for the first-year teacher as well. Children growing up in unconventional families—families with two mothers or those going through a heated divorce and custody battle, for example—may have special needs or sensitivities unfamiliar to the beginning teacher as well.

"I knew the first year would be difficult," writes one beginning teacher, "but I didn't expect all of the pressures of dealing with at-risk students on top of the pressures of being a first-year teacher" (Pearson & Honig, 1992, p. 7). In the San Diego study, 13 of 15 new teachers interviewed reported extreme discomfort with ethnic friction and sexual behavior among students, and all 15 agreed that "their lack of understanding of the different social and cultural behaviors of their students made both planning and instruction very difficult" (Mathison, 1996, p. 12). Whereas diversity within the classroom can be enriching, then, it also adds to the layers of challenge for the beginning teacher trying to reach all students.

Student Motivation

Many teachers fear that their students will not be receptive to their instruction and will refuse to learn. In fact, this fear is often valid (Wilson et al., 1997, p. 399). In the San Diego study, 6 of 15 new teachers complained that the students' lack of motivation "to do anything" was particularly demoralizing (Mathison, 1996, p. 13). The problem is compounded when it comes to students who have special needs. These students, even more than others, are often afraid to take risks and constantly fear that they will fail. Inability to motivate special-needs students and others can cause anxiety for the teacher; discussing this anxiety with a more experienced teacher may alleviate it.

A Solitary Work Environment

One of the great challenges of teaching is the loneliness in the classroom and the presence of what can be, at times, an awful feeling of isolation. Teachers entering the profession have rarely thought about the fact that most instructors—at virtually all levels—are alone with students most of the school day. Once in their own classroom, however, they rarely have the opportunity to observe other teachers in action or to turn to another professional when a question arises. From the beginning, they are the sole professionals in their domain. Without the specific assignment of a mentor to work with them, they may find themselves completely independent of all other adults in their new career.

Relationships With Parents and Colleagues

Worries about meetings with parents are common among beginning teachers, often because these teachers fear confrontation. Conferences can be intimidating, especially the first time (Wilson et al., 1997, p. 397). Conversely, parents' lack of interest can be discouraging. Beginning teachers often need help preparing for their first back-to-school night, open house, regular parent-teacher conferences, and special conferences called by the beginning teacher or the parents to discuss problems (Jonson, 1999a). When the parental conference is likely to be emotionally charged, too, the beginning teacher can benefit greatly from a veteran's suggestions.

Fitting in with and gaining acceptance from peers can also be a challenge. As beginning teachers learn to negotiate the social realities of the faculty room, they often butt up against the old norms of individualism, isolationism, and privatism. For a mentor-mentee relationship to be successful, mentors must be selected because they are on the cusp of change in school culture, in an ideal position to forgo individual work for joint work. They must model the values of collegiality, openness, and trust over detachment and territoriality. In so doing, they will help beginning teachers develop new ways of doing business and of viewing themselves and their profession.

CONCLUSION

Most beginning teachers find themselves in culture shock soon after starting their professional careers; often their preservice training (if they had any) has not prepared them adequately for the real challenges of their profession. Classroom management and discipline are only two of the issues of concern to these beginners. It is important for mentors to think back to their own early years and remember the issues that they worried about then.

Chapter 4 looks at the many skills required of any teacher: teaching, interpersonal, and coping skills. Just as an effective mentor needs to remember early anxieties, he also needs to continually refer back to these basic skills.

> New teachers yearn for a sense of professional rootedness and community. Too often, however, they know only a sense of dislocation and loneliness, of compromise and inadequacy—feelings that cause them to question their commitment to school life. . . . Many beginning teachers find themselves in school systems that are ill-prepared to welcome them appropriately. These beginners are isolated professionally and socially. They join aging and habit-bound faculties whose members already know the ropes. They become the have-nots among the haves, the ones with neither the tricks of the trade nor with wisdom of experience. (Moran, 1990, pp. 210-211)

4

Getting Off to a Good Start

Miss Jacobs, a new teacher at Central Elementary, is planning a required unit on volcanoes as part of her third-grade science curriculum. She has three weeks to teach the unit. Miss Jacobs's favorite subject is science, and she is excited about working with her class on this unit. She still remembers an experiment she did related to the topic when she was a child, although she can't remember exactly how old she was at the time.

At Central Elementary, all third-grade teachers use a standard science textbook, which includes a unit on the topic of volcanoes. Miss Jacobs does not like the book and is particularly unenthusiastic about this chapter, but she's been told she must use it. Mr. Bennett, another third-grade teacher, has suggested that she assign supplementary reading material as well if she would like, but she's not sure that the children will do both, and she wants to leave time for activities other than reading.

In addition to assigning and discussing the reading, Miss Jacobs would like to have her students do the hands-on experiment she remembers from her childhood. Also, Mr. Bennett has just told her that the local public library, within walking distance, has a special exhibit on volcanoes. He has suggested that she mention it to her students in case any of them would like to go see it after school someday. She wonders out loud why the two classes can't go on a field trip to see the exhibit. Mr. Bennett agrees that the students might learn a lot from the experience but says he doesn't have time to coordinate it. Miss Jacobs volunteers to organize it and make plans for both classes.

Miss Jacobs has two students in her classroom with learning disabilities and one who is pulled out for speech class on Tuesdays and Thursdays. Three of her students struggle with their reading and often need help with textbook assignments. She also has a student in the gifted program and another who seems to have an exceptional aptitude for science. She has already arranged with the librarian for the field trip and okayed the date with Mr. Bennett when she passes the speech teacher in the hall and realizes suddenly that the scheduled date will conflict with speech pullout.

Miss Jacobs has 20 students in her class and a small, portable classroom with little extra space. Desks are currently arranged in rows, facing the front. For the science experiment she has planned, students will need to work together in groups of four on a project that will require a large amount of space. Furthermore, one phase of the project, involving papier-mâché, will need to dry overnight, so the space will need to be designated for a few days.

Miss Jacobs wants to start the unit with a discussion, followed by in-class reading time. But the students read at different paces, so she must be sure to have something to occupy the fast readers. She also knows from previous projects that her gifted student has great ideas but tends to irritate some of the other children when working in small groups because she doesn't like to listen to their ideas. Most of the kids have difficulty beginning a project in small groups, and several will need constant supervision if they are to remain on task.

Because it is flu season in her community, absenteeism at Central Elementary is high. Miss Jacobs fills out daily attendance records, but she also needs to keep close track of who has been at school for what part of the science project so she can make sure those who are ill can somehow make up the work and gain the understanding they need in time for later parts of the project. Because she has decided to base much of their grade on their participation in conducting the experiment, she needs to have a way to monitor that participation and provide makeup opportunities.

Miss Jacobs is pleased to find a six-page article in a children's magazine, including lots of color illustrations, that covers most of the same information about volcanoes as the textbook but in a more interesting way; she can supplement with discussion, she thinks. Mr. Bennett insists that she must use the standard text, however. She wonders if he's right about this but doesn't want to offend him by questioning too much. Also, she doesn't know if she can photocopy the pages to give to the students. If she can, she'll need to ask about the procedure. If not, she'll need to figure out a way for everyone to read the original.

She also needs to find out about school policies regarding field trips. Permission slips go home with the children, and she sends out interest forms to all the parents in her class and in Mr. Bennett's class to find chaperones. When the forms come back, she finds that she is one adult short of the required ratio. In addition, she vaguely remembers that a second-grade teacher has warned her not to allow one of her parent volunteers, Mr. Smith, to have sole responsibility for any of the kids. She can't remember why not or who told her or even for certain if Mr. Smith is the correct person.

On a trial walk to the library, Miss Jacobs realizes that the group will need to cross two very busy streets en route. She wants to telephone a few parents to ask them directly if they could possibly help chaperone the field trip, but she doesn't know any of them and doesn't want to put anyone on the spot. She wonders if she should talk with Mr. Smith in particular about watching the kids closely, especially considering she won't have any extra adults, but she doesn't want to seem mistrusting. She wishes she could remember who warned her about Mr. Smith and what the problem was.

She also wishes that Mr. Bennett would help her more with planning this field trip and finds herself becoming short-tempered with him, though she reminds herself that she did volunteer. She is just wondering if she should cancel the trip when she finds a note from Mr. Bennett saying that one of his parents has volunteered late to go along, so the trip is legal, and he's looking forward to it. The day before the volcano project is to begin, Miss Jacobs gives away tickets she has to a concert that night and works long hours preparing so she will be ready for the unit.

The next morning, she is eager to begin but also somewhat discouraged. Despite her good intentions, she never did talk to anyone about the textbook and ends up assigning the reading from it despite her wishes. As she predicted, some of the kids are uninterested and spend their reading time talking with each other and drawing pictures in their notebooks. When she reminds them to get back to work, one informs her that the book is boring.

The night before the field trip, she can't sleep. She has met her legal quota for chaperones, but she wonders if she should have gotten extra adults given the busy street crossings and Mr. Smith's shaky record.

Miss Jacobs wishes the project were over. She should have followed the suggestions of the other third-grade teachers, she thinks, and just had the kids read and answer questions. She hopes the kids will be excited about the experiment, but she no longer has faith that they will be. She hopes it won't be too hard for them and wishes she had thought more about that beforehand. Perhaps she should have left an extra half hour to work on it. But then they would be late to music class.

She thinks maybe she'll do something easier for the next unit.

While much of designing a lesson may be second nature for the experienced teacher, the process is not so natural for the novice. Even the beginning teacher with original ideas, like Miss Jacobs, may have difficulty working all the pieces together to maximize learning for the variety of students in the classroom. In addition to drawing from teaching skills, the teacher must use a variety of interpersonal skills to enlist the help of others at the school and perhaps to solicit parent involvement. A beginning teacher may well need assistance juggling everything to keep from becoming discouraged.

An effective mentor should not only understand the fears of a beginning teacher, then, but also review the basics of teaching required at all levels of experience and be prepared to assist the mentee with suggestions and support. A good mentor should be aware of the mentee's skills, attempt to help the beginning teacher develop proficiency, and provide encouragement when things do not seem to be working.

Support for the beginning teacher falls broadly into three categories of required abilities: *teaching skills* (planning lessons, working with students, managing the classroom, and dealing with administrative tasks); *interpersonal skills* (working with colleagues and other school personnel, dealing with parents, adhering to school policy, and supporting the school and the district); and *coping skills* (balancing work time with personal time, learning from colleagues, managing stress, and continuing professional development).

TEACHING SKILLS

Of all the skills required, the basics of teaching are most likely to have been covered thoroughly in preservice credential courses. Even so, the beginning teacher may have difficulty putting theory to practice in the classroom and adapting what she has learned to her specific situation. Both the variety of students at a particular work site and the policies of the system could affect outcome, even with the most careful preparation.

Miss Jacobs, for example, had to draw on a wide variety of teaching skills to plan her lessons for the unit on volcanoes. She needed to figure out how to work with students of varying abilities in her classroom, how to set up the classroom so that the experiment could be done successfully, and how to assess her students' learning. Administrative tasks for this unit included obtaining permission slips and chaperones for the field trip.

Lesson Planning

Effective teaching depends on effective lesson planning. To maximize both student learning and appropriate classroom behavior, teachers must thoughtfully and carefully prepare for every minute with the students.

This task can be overwhelming for the beginner. Whereas a seasoned teacher can draw from past experience and adapt previously prepared lessons, the beginning teacher must develop everything from the start. The veteran teacher has an idea about what will and what won't work, but the novice has only theory to work with.

Developing strategies for effective teaching is a continuous process, with an ongoing learning curve for all teachers. Throughout this process, the teacher must link curriculum, specific instruction, and assessment to standards-based learning. To be effective, the teacher needs to be able to

1. Develop instructional strategies and methods
   a. Cover essential core curriculum over the course of the year
   b. Schedule each day and week to address all subject areas within the given time frames
   c. Plan daily lessons and thematic units
   d. Constantly align lesson objectives with standards to be addressed
   e. Maximize time spent on learning

2. Select curriculum materials, again keeping standards in mind at all times

3. Perform assessments (formative, diagnostic, summative, formal, and informal)

Developing Instructional Strategies. A mentor can help the beginning teacher to keep in mind the primary goals of lesson planning: to maximize time spent on academic subjects and to manage the classroom so that students are engaged, on task, and achieving success. To accomplish these goals, the teacher needs to motivate students by keeping the lessons interesting. In addition, he needs to continually relate instruction to standards. A form such as the one in Figure 4.1 might help in planning instructional units.

If a beginning teacher is struggling with a unit or complains that students are not interested, a mentor should consider whether that teacher is using a variety of strategies for teaching. She could suggest different techniques for getting a point across, perhaps suggesting alternative activities to help the beginning teacher think about a strategy that might be more effective (see Box 4.1). By brainstorming together, the two might come up with a lesson that deals with the curriculum but that is more interesting and effective.

One critical problem many beginning teachers (and some veterans) have is identifying what they want students to know and be able to do and determining how they will know that students have learned it. With this in mind, the mentor can help the beginning teacher plan lessons, assess student learning, find ways to provide enrichment for those students who have the concept, and find ways to provide supplementation for those

(text continues on page 55)

Figure 4.1. Unit Planning Form

I. Duration (dates and times):_____

II. Students (grade level):_____
    Student Characteristics:

    _____

    _____

III. Unit Topic or Theme: _____

IV. Subjects: _____

V. Unit Objectives (incorporate required standards):_____

    _____

    _____

    _____

VI. Materials and Media (curriculum books, materials, and resources
    to be used): _____

    _____

    _____

    _____

    _____

VII. Procedures/Instructional Activities
    A. Introduction (procedure for introducing the unit):_____

        _____

        _____

        _____

Figure 4.1. Continued

    B. Content and Activities (at least six lesson topics, with prelimi-nary notes on content, teaching strategies, activities, and assignments for each): _____

_____

_____

_____

_____

_____

_____

_____

    C. Culminating Activity: _____

_____

_____

_____

_____

_____

VIII. Evaluation (indicators for success, procedure[s] for assessment of learner understanding): _____

_____

_____

_____

_____

Box 4.1

Activities to Use for Instruction

- Instructing the entire class
- Leading whole-class discussions
- Organizing small-group discussions
- Having students do activities in small groups
- Arranging for a resource person to visit
- Allowing time for students to work independently on projects
- Having students write in journals
- Going on a field trip
- Listening to tapes
- Making models
- Making charts, diagrams, posters, maps, or graphs
- Having students give oral reports
- Telling stories
- Having students dramatize or role-play
- Playing instructional games
- Making bulletin boards
- Making displays
- Viewing films, videos, or slides
- Having students do library research
- Having a panel discussion
- Having demonstrations
- Having students sing or perform finger plays
- Encouraging high-level thinking through specific questions
- Using hands-on engaged student learning
- Using cooperative learning strategies such as jigsaw puzzles or a team games tournament
- Using problem-based learning
- Using technology for Internet research, keypals, and other online learning projects
- Using teacher-made graphic organizers or having students make their own graphic organizers
- Using reciprocal teaching
- Using differentiated assignments
- Using inductive teaching strategies such as concept attainment
- Using scaffolding prior to assigning silent reading

who don't quite "get it." On the other hand, a teacher such as Miss Jacobs, who already has ideas, may simply need encouragement and help with logistics—or she might benefit from suggestions for additional activities. A more experienced teacher might suggest that Miss Jacobs have students write in their journals, for example, to help them think about what they are learning. This could also serve as a tool for Miss Jacobs to use in tracking student progress.

Obtaining Curriculum Materials. Beginning teachers are often at a disadvantage in that they lack a supply of materials to select from to reinforce coursework. A veteran teacher has likely built a collection through the years of colorful posters to enliven the room and supplement lessons, books to stock a classroom library, and other supplies. Sharing surplus materials can go a long way toward enhancing the beginning teacher's curriculum. A mentor who does not have materials suitable for the mentee may know of another teacher who does. Suggesting read-aloud books or supplementary reading materials that have proven popular with students through the years can also be a big help (see Box 4.2). Offering tips for building book collections—perhaps through dividends from commercial book club orders, for example—would be another good service to the beginning teacher. Suggesting online resources—Web sites, listservs, chat groups, and newsletters—would also be helpful.

Developing Assessment Tools and Techniques. Teachers have many options for assessing student progress and achievement, some formal and others informal. Some forms of assessment relate specifically to the particular classroom and are in the hands of the teacher. The goal of classroom

---

Box 4.2

2,700 Good Books to Read

In July 2001, the California State Department of Education posted on the Internet an updated list of recommended works of fiction, nonfiction, poetry, and drama for kindergarten through Grade 12. The comprehensive index replaces versions released in 1990 and 1996 and can be accessed by various search categories, including grade level, genre, and language. There are titles in English, Spanish, Hmong, Vietnamese, Chinese, and Filipino/Tagalog. Synopses are included in annotations, which may also suggest links to a particular state reading standard or mention what the department calls "sensitive subject matter." Find it at www.cde.ca.gov/ci/literature

assessment is not only to determine the student's ability to perform in a given subject area but also to monitor and adjust teaching. These assessments might be based on culminating exhibitions or presentations, writing samples, portfolios (collections of work showing development in progress), classroom observations over a period of time, questionnaires and surveys, or oral questions and interviews.

Good mentors can help beginning teachers by sharing techniques commonly used at their school and by discussing school policies about assessment. The mentor can also make sure that the beginning teacher has a procedure in place for evaluating and determining grades. The beginning teacher might even benefit from a general discussion about the purposes of assessment: to obtain information on student progress to report to parents, to learn where instructional planning needs improvement, and to make students aware of their strengths.

One of the most formal types of assessment, commercial standardized tests, is usually required of all children in a given system. Beginning teachers need to understand what is on these tests, how they are to be administered, and what to communicate about them to parents or older students. They need to understand the purposes of standardized testing and to be able to analyze the data from these tests. After analysis, a mentor may be able to assist the beginning teacher in planning instruction that will help individuals who lack the skills or in planning extensions for enrichment of students who score high on the tests. Even on a logistical level, beginning teachers or teachers new to a district may need help with assessment timelines and procedures for district- or state-mandated assessments. Mentors can make sure that these new teachers understand the requirements, procedures, and conditions of testing.

Working With Students

A skilled teacher reaches all students, from struggling and special-needs students to gifted learners. As in Miss Jacobs's case, a class may include students who need to be pulled out at times for a variety of reasons—from speech therapy to remedial reading—as well as some who need special attention within the classroom (because they have trouble learning or because they learn quickly and require enrichment). An effective teacher will

1. Address the individual needs of individual students
   a. Assess resources for students
   b. Allow for specialists and pullout classes
   c. Assist a child who has been pulled out or absent in re-entering the classroom afterward

2. Motivate and engage students in active learning

Addressing Individual Needs. A good teacher respects all students and treats all fairly. In addition, she works with individuals regardless of their special needs. A mentor can help the beginning teacher learn about resources available within the school to help with special needs and about school policy regarding pullout students. Through observation and experience, a mentor may also help beginning teachers become aware of individual students needing extra assistance. Without experience, the beginning teacher may fail to recognize that a student is struggling because he *can't* understand the lesson, not because he is not trying.

Gifted children also often need special attention. A teacher must learn to recognize and meet the needs of a gifted student who has shut down and is not performing. The teacher must also recognize that a child who is gifted in one area may not be gifted in another. A mentor can help the beginning teacher know where to go in the school system for additional help with resources or testing for gifted children or simply to consult with an expert.

Motivating Students. Most teachers have an ongoing concern regarding student motivation. If students are not motivated to learn, classroom management becomes a problem, and valuable lesson time is lost to discipline. If students *are* motivated, time on task increases, and learning improves.

Students will want to learn if the curriculum is interesting and the classroom enjoyable. They will rise to a lesson that is challenging and for which a variety of activities has been planned and a variety of materials introduced. A positive, personable teacher will also inspire students, and occasional rewards can be well worth the investment for achieving results. A student who feels comfortable with the learning situation is most likely to feel free to learn, grow, and change.

Here again, the mentor can help by suggesting to the beginning teacher ways to keep a lesson varied and exciting and an environment pleasant. An observant mentor may be able to see whether the classroom is encouraging to the students and, if not, to offer suggestions for improvement. The mentor might also want to help the beginning teacher concerned about lack of student motivation to evaluate the classroom. Together, the two could review and reflect on the following questions:

- Is the room physically attractive and inviting to students? Are interest centers, bulletin boards, students' desks, tables, and furniture arranged in a pleasant manner that is conducive to learning? Are books, learning materials, wall displays, pictures, and charts interesting, and are they changed regularly? Might a plant or a small pet make the room more inviting?

- Are students involved in decision making? Do they get to make choices regarding daily routine, themes, or topics of study?

- Are students encouraged to participate in a range of activities and projects? Are lessons appropriate for multiple intelligences and learning modalities?

- Are students who finish assignments early kept challenged and given the opportunity to work on additional activities, such as special projects, computer practice, free reading, and so on? Are these projects meaningful and not simply designed to keep the quick achiever busy?

- Is student work displayed throughout the room? Is it changed regularly? Do students feel successful and proud of their work?

- Are students praised for their efforts and sometimes rewarded? Are parents and other students notified of exceptional work?

- Are students encouraged routinely with smiles or kind words? Are they listened to? Complimented?

- Are students asked questions about their interests and experiences? Do they know the teacher cares?

- Do students understand why they are learning the material?

Students learn best when they feel they are in a safe, accepting environment. Reviewing the classroom setting and atmosphere can help the beginning teacher provide such an environment.

Classroom Management

The distance between theory and reality is greater when it comes to classroom management than for any other single area of teaching. New teachers often find themselves ill-prepared for this aspect of the profession and are shocked at the difficulties they encounter when they get into their first professional assignment. Managing the class effectively can sometimes seem impossible. The goals in this area are to

1. Organize the physical space of the classroom

2. Provide a safe and orderly learning environment

3. Establish effective classroom discipline systems

Organizing Physical Space. Every teacher must give careful thought to where and how students are seated in the classroom. Are they to be at individual desks in rows, or in table groups? Teaching style affects seating plans. For example, will the children be working often in small groups— or will they most often work individually or as a large group? If they are seated in groups, are the groups arranged at random, or do children choose where to sit? Will the teacher mix them by ability? Or divide them by ability? How many children to a group? Do some children need to be closer to the front of the classroom so they can hear or see well? Does a certain child need a supportive friend nearby to bring out her best? Must another child be separated from friends with whom he might chatter? Where can a child who has difficulty working in close proximity to others sit? Frequent changes in group assignments encourage students to work with and get to know a broader range of children and allow for problems to be worked out through the year.

Aside from student desks, other aspects of the physical arrangement of the classroom must be addressed. Where is the teacher to sit? Is the teacher's desk easily accessible? Is there a central meeting place in the room as well—especially for younger children? If so, can the children sit comfortably, positioned so that all can see and hear each other? Lack of attention in group activities could be caused by the children's inability to participate fully, not by their lack of interest. Is a black- or whiteboard nearby? Can a chart or a sample be positioned within view of every child?

Where will items be stored in the classroom? Where is the pencil sharpener? A classroom library? Is the library inviting? Will children want to go there in their free time? How will bulletin boards be used?

All of these things will affect the way students learn and their comfort within the classroom. Especially if space is limited, it might take some experimenting to establish the setting most conducive to learning.

Providing a Safe and Orderly Learning Environment. Children like a predictable environment, a consistent classroom with dependable routines. At the elementary school level, a morning routine allows children to start their day comfortably and should include an agenda for activities planned throughout the day. Morning rituals might include a song, a reading, journal writing, or other age-appropriate activities. For secondary students, a routine at the beginning of each period helps keep them on track. The secondary teacher might begin each period by collecting and reviewing homework, answering questions, or having students write in journals or read quietly, for example. A veteran teacher is sure to have other grade-appropriate suggestions as well.

Classroom management style varies from teacher to teacher, depending on personality and individual preferences, the age group of the students, and, with older groups, the subject matter. Some teachers conduct mostly teacher-led whole-class instruction and discussions, whereas others rely more on small-group activities. Some tolerate less noise than others, some require more order than others, and so on.

The beginning teacher must establish any class routines, rules, and procedures she chooses to implement during the first few days of school. Many teachers enlist the help of their students to set "the rules" and then post them throughout the year; others come the first day with predetermined guidelines. Depending on the age group, rules could be as simple as "Try your best" or "Organize your space." One secondary teacher states simply, "Act appropriately"—and spends a good half hour at the beginning of the year discussing the word *appropriately*. Signals for quiet should be clear to the students from the beginning. Clapping hands, whispering directions, or turning out the lights are only a few of the techniques teachers use to signal silence. Routines should be spelled out, whether they regard speaking during discussions, using the restroom, or turning in homework. Explaining to students why rules are necessary might help with later enforcement. A mentor can help with specific details about schoolwide rules and policies.

Establishing Effective Classroom Discipline Systems. Experienced teachers are more likely to mention classroom management and discipline as their most difficult problems during their first years of teaching than anything else. Even in classrooms where students are generally well behaved, occasional problems arise. Through the years, effective teachers develop strategies for dealing with problems, but beginning teachers may struggle for some time as they search to find what works for them.

Consequences for breaking the class rules should be clear to students from the beginning, just as the rules themselves should be clear from Week 1. Consequences work best if they are explained ahead of time and are specific and appropriate for the action. A mentor can help the beginning teacher make sure that her consequences are in line with school policies. Are time-outs in the hallway acceptable? Can students be kept in at recess or after school?

Most effective discipline is logical and appropriate. Children who run should go back to walk, for example. Children who write on desks should clean all desks during recess. A secondary student might be required to serve detention after school following tardiness or might have to attend study hall to make up missing assignments. Time-out may well provide an opportunity for misbehaving children to think about their actions and decide to behave appropriately. Again, a detention for a secondary student may serve the same purpose.

A mentor can help a beginning teacher see when consequences are working and when they are not. If students are misbehaving, examination of classroom management and curriculum may reveal the solution. If rules are not clear enough, they may need to be changed or clarified.

With experience, the teacher learns not only to handle problems effectively but also to prevent them in the first place; preventing a problem is always better than dealing with it after it occurs. If students are not on task, perhaps the activities are too simple or too difficult. Maybe a different seating arrangement would work better. Sometimes an experienced colleague is just the person to look objectively at a situation and help the flustered novice gain the perspective to deal with a situation appropriately.

Administrative Tasks

Even veteran teachers often struggle to find time for the huge amounts of paperwork that come across their desks. For a novice, the piles can be overwhelming. The sheer amount is one problem; understanding all the forms is another. Aside from actual teaching, teachers are responsible for

1. Keeping records

2. Grading

3. Understanding and following school policies and procedures

Paperwork falls roughly into two categories: (1) teaching related (class plans, records of student accomplishment, assessment tools, and so on) and (2) non-teaching related (forms related to school and district policies, attendance sheets, memos, meeting agendas and minutes, and so on). Researchers at the Beginning Teacher Evaluation Study, conducted by Far West Laboratory, found that elementary teachers devoted 60% of their day to academic activities, 23% to nonacademic activities, and 17% to noninstructional activities. School district researchers in Austin, Texas, followed 227 students through an entire school day and found that the students spent more than 20% of their time in noninstructional activities. Further, subtracting lunch and recess times, only 3.75 hours—about 60% of the day—was left for instruction. Similarly, a study by Michigan State University's Institute for Research on Teaching found that 27% to 42% of the elementary school day is spent in noninstructional activity. Students in classrooms with the most noninstructional activities received the equivalent of 5.5 weeks less instruction than did other classes during the same number of days (Northwest Regional Educational Laboratory, 1986, pp. 327-328, 351-352).

Keeping Records. Relying on memory when it comes time to produce report cards can be extremely dangerous. Although a teacher might expect to remember the details of a student's progress and achievement, the specifics often vanish when it comes time to assign a grade. Students blur, activities blur, and what seemed clear when it happened is very unclear after time has passed. Careful record keeping will help the teacher make insightful comments and will be useful if a student or parent challenges a grade.

Grading. If records have been carefully kept and ongoing assessments performed, grading will be much easier than if these preliminary steps have not been carried out. Still, a beginning teacher may struggle, especially with students whose work is inconsistent. When comments are written along with grades on report cards or papers, a "second set of eyes" can raise important questions of logic or tone. Does the comment make sense?

Is its meaning clear? Is it written in a way that will be constructive and not offensive? Beginning teachers may need to be reminded that a written comment is permanent and must always be well thought out and carefully worded.

Following School Policies. Understanding school policies is absolutely essential for any teacher. Policies govern everything from discipline to assessment to field trips to special-needs students. Even attendance taking can become a beginning teacher's nightmare, with specific forms required each day. In addition, middle and high school teachers must participate in house/team meetings and shared responsibilities, work with department heads and the rest of the department, and so on.

A beginner may not always know where to turn with policy questions or even when a specific policy might apply. Miss Jacobs was unsure of textbook requirements for her unit, for example, and also needed to find out the requirements for leading a field trip. A veteran teacher is often able to answer such questions easily, advising the novice when a policy might be in question or finding someone else who can help.

INTERPERSONAL SKILLS

Fitting in with the school and district culture can be a challenge for the beginning teacher. Often the teacher is new to the community as well as to the faculty and needs to build a network of people to work with. Among the interpersonal skills required at the start are

1. Building collegiality with teaching peers
2. Establishing good working relationships with other staff
3. Creating a partnership with parents
   a. Communicating
   b. Conferencing
4. Understanding and carrying out the school philosophy
5. Working on school and district projects *without becoming overwhelmed*

In setting up her unit on volcanoes, for example, Miss Jacobs needed to work with her peer, Mr. Bennett; to schedule around the speech therapist and art teacher; and to work with parents who might chaperone the field trip. All of these tasks required her interpersonal skills.

Colleagues

Gaining acceptance in a new school can take time—for the seasoned teacher new to the school as well as for a teacher just beginning in the profession. A mentor can introduce the new teacher to peers, encouraging contact with those who are positive and helpful and steering away from those likely to be more negative. Miss Jacobs, for example, needed to know where to turn to find answers about school policies regarding textbooks and copying and wasn't sure that Mr. Bennett's advice was accurate. A mentor might have been able to answer her questions or at least to get the help of someone who could. A mentor might also invite a beginning teacher with her to teacher social hours, union meetings, classes or workshops offered by the district, or other district grade-level networking opportunities.

Other School Staff

The principal, secretaries, custodial staff, volunteers, teacher aides, and resource specialists are all part of the school network. Communicating with these people is essential to varying degrees, and getting along with them can only make the teacher's job easier. A mentor can introduce the new teacher to these people and point out quirks and issues of concern to them. For example, how do custodians like the room to look at the end of the day? Who deals with spills or with necessary repairs? In what ways can parent volunteers help? How does one obtain help from a volunteer? Does the school have an established volunteer program, or does the teacher solicit help independently? What teacher aides might be available in the school? What about resource specialists? How does one obtain help from them?

Parents

Parents of the students in a classroom can either support or undermine a new teacher; they can be a great help as volunteers in the classroom and can give insight to their children, or they can create tension by hovering and criticizing. Some may be indifferent, hostile, or even belligerent. Knowing this, many new teachers worry about parents or even feel threatened by the parent community. Many other parents are interested, cooperative, and supportive, however. Even most parents who appear critical only want the best for their children. It is important to remember that parents and teachers are working toward the same goal: quality education for their children.

A mentor can discuss with the beginning teacher how other teachers in the school develop partnerships with parents. How do they get parents involved? A teacher new to the community as well as to the school may need to spend time getting to know the region so that she can better understand the parents. What are the backgrounds and values of the families in the community? What ethnic and cultural groups are represented? What is the economic base?

Communicating. Every teacher needs to make the effort to communicate with parents, to draw them into the program as allies from the beginning. The beginning teacher has no grace period in acquiring this skill; parents expect professional communications from the novice just as from the veteran. In some cases, a translator may even be required to help communicate with non-English-speaking parents.

A carefully worded letter sent home on the first day of school can go a long way toward building parent-teacher relationships (see Figures 4.2 and 4.3). A mentor can help with wording that is appropriate for the specific community and age group and can also help with proofreading. It is very important that this introductory letter, as well as all other communications, be professional. If the teacher is working with children of parents who do not speak English, the help of a translator will be necessary. In some cases, especially among some cultural groups, parent response might be better if a phone call is made rather than a letter sent. Again, the help of a translator might be necessary, and a mentor might have suggestions for resources in this area. More personal notes, phone calls, weekly newsletters, back-to-school night, open houses, and conferences provide other means of and opportunities for communication.

A request for parents to write about their child shows interest in hearing from the parents and may provide valuable information to the teacher. Questions to ask might be designed to find out what the parents would like the teacher to know about their child, how the child spends time at home, and what the parents expect of their child.

Conferencing. The parent-teacher conference is the most common means of sharing information between school and home. Careful preparation for the conference will make it go more smoothly. The mentor should encourage the new teacher to write observation notes in the weeks preceding the conference, perhaps filling out a form such as that in Figure 4.4.

When preparing for his first conference, the novice teacher should be reminded of the purposes of the conference: (a) to get information, (b) to give information, (c) to joint problem-solve, (d) to develop mutual trust, and (e) to set goals. The tone should be positive and the schedule adhered to. Mentor modeling or role playing could help things go smoothly. Discussing problem children in advance—before going to a parent with the issue—could also be very important. In addition, the mentor might

(text continues on page 68)

Figure 4.2. Sample Letter Home to Parents (Elementary School Level)

[Date]

Dear Parents,

I'm excited to be starting this school year at [school name], and I look forward to sharing a successful year with your child. [Level] grade has many new and exciting experiences in store. Together we can share in the growth and development of your child.

It would be helpful if your child could bring the following items to school:

[list items]

Please clearly mark your child's name on all clothes, supplies, and personal items.

If at any time you have questions or concerns, feel free to contact me. Also, let me know if you could help out on occasion with special activities, field trips, or [other]. I look forward to meeting you at our Back-to-School Night on [date]. If you need to contact me before that time, send a note or call me at [phone number] [when].

Sincerely,

[Teacher]

Figure 4.3. Sample Letter Home to Parents (Middle School Level)

[Date]

Dear Parents,

My name is [name], and I will be your child's [subject] teacher this year. I'm writing not only to introduce myself, but to welcome you to the [school name] family.

I am a new teacher in the [name] School District who has recently graduated from [university]. I studied [subject area] and am interested in teaching students about [state what].

I've attached a general information sheet for you and your child to read. If you have any questions or comments about it, please note them when you sign the tear-off portion. I'll be happy to meet with you in person or talk with you on the phone. Generally, I will be available [state time].

I have many ideas for projects and activities. [State a few.] Some of them will require help. I hope that some of you will have time to work with us in planning and carrying them out. I look forward to working with you so that together we can help your child have a happy, successful time in [school name].

Sincerely,

[Teacher]

[Note: On the general information sheet, include information on your classroom rules and expectations, grading policy, and homework requirements.]

Figure 4.4. Sample Form for Fall Conference Notes (Elementary)

Child's name:_____

Persons attending conference:_____

Date: _____

Student's adjustment to _____ grade:_____

_____

_____

_____

_____

_____

_____

Student's achievement relative to district standards in

      Reading:_____

      Writing:_____

      Math:_____

      Social Studies: _____

      Science:_____

      Art, PE, Computer, Music (as appropriate): _____

Interaction with peers: _____

Interaction with adults: _____

Favorite friends: _____

Greatest strength: _____

Area needing most support: _____

Follow-up: _____

_____

_____

suggest ways for the beginning teacher to partner with parents, such as asking parents for information about their child's learning styles and interests, areas that are difficult for the child, suggestions about handling the child's behavior, and so on. In secondary schools, the mentor could work with the beginning teacher to prepare for student-led conferences.

School Philosophy

Most schools today have developed a philosophy or vision statement that is worth reviewing and discussing. Both beginning teachers and teachers new to a district need to think about their personal fit with the school's philosophy and goals. This issue has grown in importance as social changes have altered the landscape of classrooms. Will the new teacher be able to work with the school's diverse population of students and parents? Will the new teacher devote the necessary time and energy to planning and working with colleagues to provide the best opportunity available for students? Can the new teacher provide an unwavering commitment to fully include *all* students; to recognize and respond to individual differences in students; to implement a variety of teaching strategies that result in high student achievement; to work cooperatively with parents, colleagues, support staff, and supervisors; and to display genuine respect for all? The school's philosophy will often make statements about such issues. New teachers must keep in mind the importance of the match between the vision of the school where they have accepted employment and their own vision of what it is they want to accomplish for children in the years ahead.

In addition, the teacher new to a school—whether a beginning teacher or a veteran—needs to be aware of specific goals in that school and be willing to work toward them. If the school has determined that all students within it should be on grade level in reading by a certain grade, for example, the teacher needs to be aware of that goal and to be willing to commit to it.

School and District Projects

Schools and districts need teachers to commit time and energy to a wide variety of projects. These include working toward school improvement goals, serving on committees, taking part in extracurricular activities, and so forth. Offering to help with such schoolwide projects is a good way for a new teacher to gain acceptance in the community—but only within limits. Overextending will only add to the frustration when daily routine itself seems too much. A good compromise would be for the new teacher to choose and become involved with one significant project. By contributing to this one project, the new teacher will prove an interest in supporting the school as a whole and will have the opportunity to network with others without sacrificing too much of her own classroom and personal time.

COPING SKILLS

Striking a balance between professional and personal time can be difficult and may even seem impossible at first. As Miss Jacobs discovered, an ambitious class project may well mean extra hours long into the night at home. Frustrations can also add to the stress. Miss Jacobs, for example, became discouraged at the lack of help she got from Mr. Bennett.

On the other hand, some teachers find themselves stressed because the work isn't getting done—but this time because they have *too much* of a social life. Some come late to school and leave early, never take anything home, and let their students correct all of their own work. A mentor needs to step in when this is happening as well, again assisting the beginner in better time management.

Although the enthusiastic new teacher may eagerly sacrifice in the beginning, he will soon wear out if not kept in check. Mentors can suggest or teach coping skills to help the beginning teacher manage better and more efficiently or can suggest workshops to help their protégés improve skills.

Miss Jacobs approached her unit on volcanoes with some wonderful ideas and a lot of enthusiasm. As the planning proceeded and she got bogged down in details, however, she began to lose her spirit. An effective mentor would have been able to help her with her questions. In some cases, her worries were about things that could have been easily addressed by a veteran. For other worries, simple encouragement would have helped keep her spirits up. Box 4.3 lists ways to improve one's coping skills.

Box 4.3

Ways for a Teacher to Improve Coping

1. Improve time management techniques
2. Learn from colleagues
3. Adapt relaxation and stress management strategies
4. Continue professional development to become a more proficient teacher

Improving Time Management

Despite insistence that there is no time for planning, a new teacher must be encouraged to *find* that time. Without scheduling both in-school and out-of-school activities, priorities may not be achieved, and the teacher will continue to feel worn out, unable to accomplish all of her goals in a day. She should identify activities, both personal and job related, to achieve her goals. The mentor can help her set priorities, estimate the time required for those activities, and establish a realistic schedule. A few minutes at the end of the day to prepare a to-do list for the next day are well worth the time.

Learning From Colleagues

A mentor can share all kinds of ideas with a beginning teacher—or put the mentee in touch with another teacher who has worked on a similar project. Even if Mr. Bennett did not help Miss Jacobs, perhaps another third-grade teacher could have—or a teacher from another grade level may have had experience planning a similar project. A mentor can direct the beginning teacher to teachers who will be receptive to questions and might also have made Mr. Bennett aware of Miss Jacobs's unapparent stress. Finally, a mentor with a history at a given site may well know which teachers have taught which grade levels in the past, regardless of their current level.

Improving Relaxation and Stress Management Strategies

If stress is related to something that the teacher can control, defining the cause can be the beginning of alleviating the problem. A teacher who is stressed by piled-up paperwork, for example, may need to make a priority of dealing with paper as it comes in. If the teacher does not know *how* to deal with the forms, a mentor aware of the problem can give assistance. If the stress is related to daily routine, a change might help: An art project in the middle of the day, for example, could break up the schedule. Even a change to the physical appearance of a room may improve the teacher's feelings.

If the source of stress is not controllable—for example, if pending conferences are the cause—other techniques might work. Some teachers use meditation or other relaxation methods, stretching, deep breathing, deep muscle massage, exercise, or a healthful diet. Whatever the choice, the beginning teacher must take time away from the job for himself, must find a balance between his professional and personal life. A treat of a movie, a sporting event, a concert, or a night out for dinner might do the trick. Some teachers purchase season tickets to a favorite event before the school year begins so they will be sure to set aside time. A mentor can encourage the beginning teacher to keep personal activities a priority, as important to her teaching career as the school routine itself.

Continuing Professional Development

Mentors should have information for their mentees about different workshops and courses available to help them improve their skills. With improved skills, particularly those relevant to the grade level or subject matter, the beginning teacher will improve efficiency and gain confidence. In some programs, mentors even have available to them funds to use to help mentees with professional development. The mentor should share information about possible available resources.

> Beginning teachers do not assume their first teaching assignments as autonomous professionals. And even some veteran teachers experience situations in which their resourcefulness is at a low ebb. Professional growth . . . occurs developmentally and individually over time. Growth is supported through mediated experiences by skilled leaders in workshops, course work, reading, study, and collaboration and modeling in the school environment. (Costa & Garmston, 1994, p. 165)

CONCLUSION

Every teacher, whether a first-year novice or a veteran of many years, must draw on a wide variety of skills to be effective. Both teaching skills and interpersonal skills are necessary for the teacher to maximize learning time for students and minimize time wasted on classroom management and discipline.

A teacher like Miss Jacobs, who uses her teaching skills to develop a strong lesson plan and her interpersonal skills to get the help she needs, may someday be outstanding in her profession—if she can keep from burning out. To keep her and other beginning teachers on track, a third set of skills—coping skills—is also required. A good mentor can help in all of these areas by providing assistance, answering questions, and offering support and encouragement.

Chapter 5 offers specific strategies for working with the mentee to build these skills.

> Relax! Only your family expects you to be perfect.
>
> —Advice from a mentor teacher

5

Strategies for Mentoring

Karen Kawasaki, a new teacher at Mt. Carmel High School, "had great lesson plans, great ideas and projects, and an interactive style of teaching," according to Charlotte Kutzner, a veteran teacher in the Poway School District where Kawasaki teaches north of San Diego. But Kawasaki had a problem. As a new teacher, she also had trouble with classroom management, and after the school principal visited her classroom a couple of times, he told her that she needed to improve. She worried that she might lose her job.

In the Poway School District, teachers with two years or less of experience are assigned to teacher consultants. Kawasaki's consultant, however, had been out on sick leave. In November, a new consultant—Kutzner—was assigned.

"I was in her classroom once or twice a week," says Kutzner. "We talked a lot. We observed veteran teachers to see how they dealt with the problem. We even role-played ideas for how to handle students at the beginning of the class."

"Charlotte helped me a lot," Kawasaki says. "She made suggestions. . . . My confidence level went up."

At the end of the year, Kawasaki's job was assured, and she is now considered an excellent teacher.

—California Teacher *(Bacon, 1997, pp. 1, 6)*

Karen Kawasaki's situation was similar to that of many beginning teachers across the country: She was doing a lot right but just couldn't figure out *everything* by herself. Unlike many beginning teachers, however, Kawasaki was fortunate enough to connect with an effective mentor who could guide her through, who was available to her, and who was able to provide her with the quality time necessary for her to work through her problems at an appropriate pace (Fraser, 1998, p. 26). Charlotte Kutzner was able to be the kind of mentor Portner (1998) describes as ideal: one who can relate to the new teacher's experience, assess her abilities, coach her as she develops new skills, and guide her to reflect on her experience (pp. 7-8).

"As consultants, we applaud what's going well, but also help teachers with their next best step," Kutzner says. "It's important to tailor assistance to the needs of the individual teacher" (Bacon, 1997, p. 7).

To get the most from their relationship, a mentor and a mentee need to plan together to determine goals that they will work toward. They should be realistic about the time they have and explicit about the things they want to work on (Stanulis & Weaver, 1998, p. 138). To help the beginning teacher reach these goals, the mentor must perform a variety of functions, ranging from observing in the classroom and providing feedback to helping the beginning teacher develop specific skills through serving as a role model in the full scope of daily professional activities (see Box 5.1).

Many of the strategies that experienced mentors find most helpful in aiding their mentees can be grouped into the following categories:

- Direct assistance
- Demonstration teaching
- Observation and feedback
- Informal contact
- Assistance with an action plan for professional growth
- Role modeling

A full description of each function follows. See Figure 5.1 for the range of mentor functions and Table 5.1 for the relative importance given to the various functions by mentors surveyed in the San Francisco School District. No matter what the strategy, however, mentors should remember that the mentor-mentee relationship becomes more personally caring and professional when their mentees perceive them as being genuinely interested—"helpful, caring, willing to take time, dedicated, friendly, outgoing, patient, influential" (Jonson, 1999b)—and as being professional role models.

Box 5.1

Strategies a Good Mentor Can Use to Help the Beginning Teacher

- Share school protocol and traditions with the new teacher
- Guide the mentee through the daily operation of the school
- Explain school procedures as appropriate
- Brainstorm with the mentee to help develop lesson plans
- Provide occasional lesson plans
- Suggest classroom management techniques
- Role-play a parent conference
- Examine student work together
- Demonstrate lessons for the mentee
- Demonstrate record keeping
- Arrange for the mentee to visit a different teacher's classroom, and discuss the observation afterward
- Observe the mentee's teaching and provide feedback
- Meet regularly with the mentee, both formally and informally
- Support and counsel the mentee, providing perspective when needed
- Ask questions to help the beginning teacher prioritize issues and concerns
- Assist the beginning teacher in developing an action plan for professional growth
- Share resources, including materials for a curriculum unit, professional readings, children's literature, and so on
- Attend a workshop together with the mentee
- Role-model all aspects of professionalism
- Encourage reflection

DIRECT ASSISTANCE

The new teacher looked distressed after school, so I engaged her in small talk for a few minutes. She then explained that a parent was giving her a hard time, and she asked me what to do about it. First, I had to let her know that it was the mother with the problem. I told her how I had handled similar problems and we came up with things she could do that are comfortable for her. She hasn't had any problems with that parent since then, but I believe she has a more positive self (teacher) image, and she feels more comfortable in dealing with unhappy parents.

—A mentor (Jonson, 1999b)

Figure 5.1. Mentor Functions

When to Use Direct Assistance

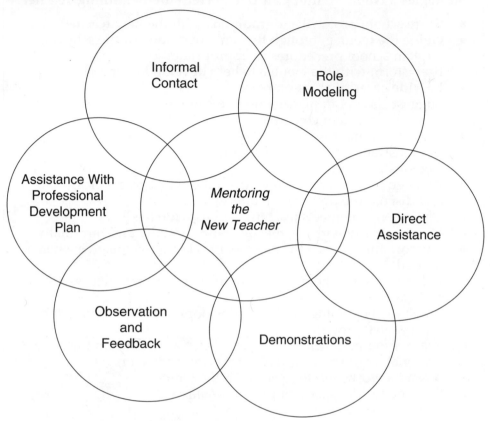

Mentor-teachers carry out many specific tasks while helping beginning teachers. Various titles apply to these tasks: behaviors, functions, roles. Though some may fall under other categories of strategies as well, all involve the mentor giving assistance in some direct way.

Because beginning teachers want to achieve professional autonomy and status equality with their colleagues, a large percentage of them do not seek help from colleagues except indirectly by swapping stories about personal experiences. This hides the weaknesses of beginners but does not enable them to obtain help with those factors—inexperience, unavailability of expertise, and ambiguity about goal attainment—that produce teacher stress related to performing professional tasks.

Beginning teachers need practical suggestions for preventing problems, solving them when they occur, and resolving conflicts and other minor emergencies. Mentors who directly assist their mentees tend to be the most helpful. In fact, mentors in the San Francisco survey ranked direct assistance as being *very useful* more often than any other function (Jonson, 1999b).

Table 5.1 The Importance of Mentoring Strategies

	Very Useful	Somewhat Useful	Not Useful	Not Practiced
Direct assistance	25	3	0	0
Demonstration teaching	18[a]	8	0	2
Observation and conferences	21[b,c]	5	0	2
Informal contact	24[d]	4	0	0
Assistance with professional growth plan	13	10	2	3
Role modeling	24[e,f]	3	1	0

SOURCE: Jonson (1999b).

NOTE: The following notes are quotes from the mentors surveyed.

a. When used to make a point.

b. If there is a trusting relationship.

c. If conferences are informal to minimize stress.

d. Informal contact may be several times/day . . . builds relationship and provides many quick "fixes" easily.

e. Useful if done before mentee takes over class. Less useful afterward because it dissipates mentee's position of authority in the eyes of the students.

f. The aspect of role modeling is not one I consciously set about doing. But, more than other areas, mentees tell me, in conversations several years later, that they wanted to "be like you." To me, it is a hidden part of mentoring. But, if the mentee doesn't feel that respect and admiration for the mentor, why would they pay attention to the mentor's ideas? I also think the respect other colleagues show for the mentor gives the mentee more reason to want to learn from the mentor.

In a classic study of first-year teachers in New York City, Sacks and Brady (1985) identified the following areas of need in which a mentor might directly assist a mentee:

- Moral support, guidance, and feedback
- Discipline and management
- Curriculum and lesson planning
- School routines and scheduling
- Motivational techniques
- Individualized instruction

Some mentors offer this help only when the mentee requests it; others step in whenever they see it as appropriate. Each mentor must personally decide when and how he will offer direct assistance.

Recommended Procedures

Mentors need to offer to share the wealth of knowledge and experience they have gained but at the same time take care not to intimidate or overwhelm. It is important that the mentor make time available on a regular basis to address the mentee's concerns and progress and to ensure interaction. Sharing the same planning period helps a great deal. Box 5.2 lists a number of ways a mentor can directly assist a mentee.

Box 5.2

Ways for a Mentor to Provide Direct Assistance

- Help the mentee organize and manage materials.
- Help the mentee develop and maintain a record-keeping system.
- Respond to specific requests by the mentee.
- Inform the mentee of workshops and other activities and opportunities for professional involvement.
- Help the mentee understand the written and unwritten rules and norms in the school and community.
- Help the mentee develop a classroom management system.
- Help the mentee develop a discipline plan.
- Assist the mentee in socializing within the school environment.
- Model or suggest techniques for conferencing with parents.
- Act as a confidant for the mentee to express personal and professional concerns.
- Help the mentee identify specific competencies that need improvement.
- Encourage and support self-direction and autonomy.
- Help the mentee assess current skills.
- Model skillful teaching strategies.
- Help the mentee diagnose students' learning styles and modify teaching strategies to meet all students' needs.
- Bring new methods, materials, and resources to the attention of the mentee and provide assistance in their implementation.

- Confer with the mentee regarding effective ways to meet student learning objectives and district instructional goals.

- Provide examples of unit plans and course syllabi.

- Give feedback on the mentee's progress in meeting instructional goals.

- Encourage the mentee in her efforts to develop her own ideas, teaching style, and classroom management plan.

- Identify resource people, such as the principal and staff development specialists (if available) in the district, along with those in district and regional support agencies.

- Assist the mentee in building competencies in areas of concern identified by the mentee's evaluator, at the request of the mentee.

- Work together with a mentee to plan an instructional unit or on some other endeavor.

DEMONSTRATION TEACHING

A wealthy woman asked a famous millinery designer to design a hat for her. He placed a canvas form on her head, and in eight minutes with a single piece of ribbon, he created a beautiful hat right before her eyes.

The matron was delighted. "How much will that be?" she asked.

"Fifty dollars," he replied.

"Why, that's outrageous," she said. "It's only a piece of ribbon!"

The milliner quickly unraveled the ribbon and, handing it to her, said, "Madame, the ribbon is free!"

—As told by Janice Watson (1992)
attributed to "Dear Abby"

A demonstration occurs when an experienced teacher shows a beginning teacher the proper use of a strategy, technique, or skill by incorporating it into an actual classroom lesson. One of the more important functions of a mentor-teacher is to prepare and teach demonstration lessons so that a mentee can observe specific techniques or materials being used. Often the beginning teacher can learn from watching how the mentor manages the class, presents curriculum, and deals with problems. At other times, the mentor might suggest another teacher to demonstrate a particular technique.

Videotapes, whether prepared locally or commercially, also can be used to demonstrate effective teaching. Videotapes offer some specific advantages, including convenience and consistency, but they cannot replace the effect of a live demonstration and subsequent conferences with the demonstrating teacher.

When to Use Demonstrations

Following are examples of appropriate times for demonstrations by a mentor-teacher:

- On request of the mentee

- Following a mentor's observation of the mentee and identification of a technique that could be useful to the mentee

- By mutual agreement

- When the mentor has a specific technique to share

- On a regularly scheduled basis

- As part of the mentee's professional development plan

Recommended Procedures

When scheduling demonstration lessons, the following procedure has been used successfully by a number of mentor/mentee teams (Jonson, 1999b).

- *Predemonstration conference.* The mentor and mentee determine the goal of the demonstration/observation and what the mentee should observe and record.

- *Demonstration.* The mentor demonstrates the preestablished lesson at the scheduled time while the mentee observes.

- *Postdemonstration conference.* The mentor and mentee review and analyze what was accomplished by the demonstration. In so doing, the mentor must remember that the idea is to help, not to threaten. The two then make plans for the mentee to practice the observed skill(s), for additional observations in the mentor-teacher's classroom, or both.

This procedure uses the pre- and postconference format advocated in the cognitive coaching model of Costa and Garmston (1994). See Chapter 6 for more information on cognitive coaching.

OBSERVATION AND FEEDBACK

> When she observed my teaching, my cooperating teacher would always offer feedback in a very positive way, even when it was critical. I never felt that what she said was threatening to me, or that sense of "Oh, no, she really hated what I did" or anything like that.
>
> —New teacher (Developmental Studies Center, 1998, p. 31)

The demanding pace of the classroom gives beginning teachers little time to monitor or reflect on their behavior. As a result, they tend to use automatic responses rather than deliberate responses to handle recurring classroom situations. A variety of studies in teacher expectations and attitudes, teacher-student relationships, student attitudes, and student learning progress have demonstrated that more effective teachers tend to be "proactive," that is, to assume and maintain the initiative in structuring classroom events. Less effective teachers tend to be more "reactive," lacking clarity of objectives and methods of reaching them and less "in charge" in their classrooms.

Observing the beginning teacher and providing feedback through a postobservation conference are important mentoring activities that can help these beginning teachers. Research findings indicate that formal observation and feedback are especially effective for improving instruction (Costa & Garmston, 1994; Hunter, 1994; Showers, 1985). Feedback provided through written critiques, descriptions of classroom interaction analysis, behavior analysis, self-critiqued videotape, and other methods can also be helpful—but the use of a conference is preferred.

Feedback based on classroom observations makes beginning teachers aware of problems and helps bring about change. Sometimes the changes are obvious and simple to make, such as altering a physical arrangement. Other changes are less obvious, and systematic feedback is needed to clarify the problem and explore ways to make appropriate changes. The mentor may find that several observation-feedback cycles are necessary to focus on the beginning teacher's patterns of calling on students and involving them in classroom discussions, for example. Additionally, the beginning teacher may need to be encouraged to attend specific professional development programs to make changes because the teaching skills are complex. In general, the value of the mentor's feedback depends on its quality and presentation. All feedback should

- Address specific, concrete behaviors or characteristics

- Be focused, nonjudgmental, and evidence based

- Be credible and presented with caring intentions and in understandable terms

- Include specific guidelines for growth
- Lead to a commitment to initiate new or expanded strategies

When a mentor observes a mentee, he must note specifically what the beginning teacher is doing, what is working well, and where guidance is needed. The idea is for the mentor to record exactly what is seen and then share observations in a way that is productive and supportive. If possible, the mentor should help the beginning teacher see which existing behaviors are successful and raise the possibility of extending those behaviors rather than switching entirely to new ones. The mentor must describe the problem(s) but allow for lots of input from the beginning teacher. Feedback conferences tend to be especially productive if the beginning teacher has jotted down questions for discussion before the conference (Developmental Studies Center, 1998, p. 31).

Observation and feedback can initially be uncomfortable for both parties. With a good, trusting, supporting relationship, however, the mentor and the mentee will be able to achieve their goals through the process. A beginning teacher in California who participated in an extensive observation process found the experience worthwhile—despite the fact that the process was rigorous, with the mentor collecting information before and during the observation, comparing the results with the state standards for the teaching profession, and sharing the results in great detail with new teachers:

> The greatest benefit for me [in the mentoring program] was to be observed by an objective party who was able to tell me the good things that I was doing and the areas where I could improve. My observer affirmed my strengths but also helped me let myself "off the hook" of perfection. I allow myself to be in a learning process—like the children in my class.
>
> —Laura Wong, new teacher (Schultz, 1999, p. 103)

When to Use Observation and Feedback

What are beginning teachers interested in having observed? When mentors ask their mentees what concerns them and what they would like the mentor to observe, record, and provide feedback about, teachers request information about two distinct categories of behaviors: their own and their students'. Behaviors can further be classified as verbal or nonverbal. Tables 5.2 through 5.5 give examples of verbal and nonverbal behaviors that teachers often want mentors to observe in the classroom (Costa & Garmston, 1994, pp. 29-31).

Table 5.2   Nonverbal Feedback Most Often Requested by Teachers
About Themselves

Description	*Example*
A. Mannerisms	Pencil tapping, hair twisting, handling coins in pocket
B. Use of time	Interruptions Transitions from one activity to another Time spent with each group Time spent getting class started, dealing with routines (such as attendance), etc. Punctuality in starting/ending times
C. Movement throughout the classroom	Favoring one side of the classroom over another Monitoring student progress and seatwork
D. Modality preference	Using balanced visual, kinesthetic, and auditory modes of instruction
E. Use of handouts	Clarity, meaningfulness, adequacy, and/or complexity of seatwork
F. Use of AV equipment	Placement, appropriateness, operation
G. Pacing	Too fast, too slow, "beating a dead horse" (tempo/rhythm)
H. Meeting diverse student needs	Considering/making allowances for: Gifted/challenged Cognitive styles Emotional needs Modality strengths Languages, cultures, etc.
I. Nonverbal feedback	Body language, gestures, proximity, eye contact Moving or leaning toward students when addressing them
J. Classroom arrangements	Furniture placement Bulletin board space Environment for learning Provision for multiple uses of space/activities

SOURCE: Costa, A. L., & Garmston, R. J. (1994). *Cognitive Coaching: A Foundation for Renaissance Schools* (p. 29). Norwood, MA: Christopher-Gordon Publishers. Reprinted by permission.

Table 5.3   Verbal Feedback Most Often Requested by Teachers
AboutThemselves

Description	*Example*
A. Mannerisms	Saying "okay," "you know," or other phrases excessively
B. Sarcasm/negative feedback	Gender reference Criticism Put-downs Intonations
C. Positive/negative feedback	Use of praise, criticism, ignoring distracting student responses
D. Response behaviors	Silence, accepting, paraphrasing, clarifying, empathizing Responding to students who give "wrong" answers
E. Questioning strategies	Posing taxonomical levels of questions Asking questions in sequences
F. Clarity of presentation	Giving clear directions Making assignments clear Checking for understanding Modeling
G. Interactive patterns	Teacher—>Student—>Teacher—>Student Teacher—>Student—>Student—>Student
H. Equitable distribution of responses	Favoring gender, language proficiency, culture, perception of abilities, placement in room, etc.
I. Specific activities/teaching strategies	Lectures, group activities, lab exercises, discussion videos

SOURCE: Costa & Garmston (1994, p. 30).

Table 5.4   Nonverbal Feedback Most Often Requested by Teachers
About Their Students

Description	*Example*
A. Attentiveness	On task/Off task Note taking Volunteering for tasks
B. Preparedness	Participation Sharing Homework Materials Volunteering knowledge
C. Movement	Negative: out of seat, squirming, fidgeting, discomfort, interfering with others Positive: following directions, transitioning, self-direction, taking initiative, consulting references/atlases/dictionaries, etc.
D. Managing materials	AV equipment Textual materials Art supplies Musical instruments Lab equipment, care of library books, returning supplies, etc.

SOURCE: Costa & Garmston (1994, p. 31).

Table 5.5   Verbal Feedback Most Often Requested by Teachers
About Their Students

Description	*Example*
A. Participating	Positive: volunteering verbal responses, speaking out—on task, student-to-student interaction—on task, requesting assistance Negative: speaking out—off task, student-to-student interaction—off task
B. Social interaction	Positive: listening, allowing for differences, sharing, establishing ground rules, assuming and carrying out roles, following rules of games, etc. Negative: interrupting, interfering, hitting, name calling, put-downs, culturally insensitive language, swearing, hoarding, stealing
C. Performing lesson objectives	Using correct terminology Applying knowledge learned before or elsewhere Performing task correctly Conducting experiments Applying rules, algorithms, procedures, formulas, etc. Recalling information Supplying supportive details, rationale, elaboration
D. Language patterns	Using correct grammar, spelling, punctuation, counting Using correct syntax Supplying examples
E. Insights into student behaviors/difficulties	Learning styles: verbal, auditory, kinesthetic, etc. Cognitive styles: field sensitive, field independent, etc. Friendships/animosities Tolerance for ambiguity/disorder Distractability

SOURCE: Costa & Garmston (1994, p. 32).

Recommended Procedure: The Formal Conference

A formal conference-and-observation cycle follows steps similar to those described for demonstrations. In this case, though, the mentee is the focus of the observations discussed.

The formal mentor observation-conference has three parts:

- Preobservation conference
- Observation
- Postobservation conference

Ideally, the mentor and the mentee engage in the formal observation-conferencing process at least once a month. They should remember that this is a collaborative decision-making process: The mentor and the mentee need to discuss and agree on each point.

Preobservation Conference

The reliability and usefulness of a classroom observation relate directly to the amount and kind of information the observer has obtained beforehand (McGreal, 1983, p. 98). During the preconference, the mentor should gather information, and both mentor and mentee should determine a focus for the observation.

Acheson and Gall (1980, p. 98) suggest the following agenda for determining goals during a preconference. They also recommend following these steps in order. By doing so, they say, mentor and mentee together identify the teacher's concerns about instruction.

- Translate the teacher's concerns into observable behaviors.
- Identify procedures for improving the teacher's instruction.
- Assist the teacher in setting self-improvement goals.
- Arrange a time for classroom observation.
- Select an observation instrument and behaviors to be recorded.
- Clarify the instructional context in which data will be recorded.

The emphasis is on tailoring the observation to collect data on matters of interest to the beginning teacher being observed.

First Observation

Observation in this case does not mean simply watching; rather, it means intentionally and methodically watching interaction between the teacher and students. It should be planned, careful, focused, and active. Once the focus has been determined at the preconference, the mentor needs to keep that focus during the observation. The more narrowly the mentor is able to focus the classroom observation, the more accurate will be the observation (McGreal, 1983, p. 102). The mentor also needs to record data during the observation to be recalled later in a postconference.

Several techniques for recording data are discussed under the heading "Tools for Observation," later in this chapter.

Postobservation Conference

During this last phase of the observation-and-conference cycle, the mentor provides feedback to help the mentee improve. The idea is for the mentor to describe what she has observed, not to place judgment. Any feedback should be in strict confidence; the mentor must not be part of the district's system of teacher evaluation, nor does the mentor discuss the performance of the beginning teacher with other staff.

Inexperienced mentors, being quite proud of their data-gathering ability and having worked hard during the observation to take notes, may be eager to tell the beginning teacher everything they have seen. Doing so, however, will make it impossible for the beginning teacher to process all of the information. Costa and Garmston (1994) offer the following tips on data reporting to help avoid this common problem:

- Sit side by side with the mentee so that the mentee can see the mentor's notes.
- Begin by having the *mentee* recollect the lesson. This gives the mentor something to build on and also helps the mentee develop self-reflecting and self-coaching skills.
- If the mentee introduces important but tangential problems or concerns during the postconference, deal with them—even if doing so means abandoning the originally planned discussion.
- Give the mentee notes to have. In some cases, it might even help to give the mentee notes *before* the postobservation meeting.

Offering feedback in positive terms will enhance trust and support and reduce anxiety. The following guidelines will help the mentor provide positive feedback:

- Focus feedback on the behavior rather than on the person.
- Provide objective feedback, and cite specific examples.
- Describe rather than judge.
- Point out specific causes and effects.
- Share ideas rather than give advice.
- Explore alternatives rather than give solutions.
- Give only the amount of feedback the receiver can use.
- Provide feedback valuable for the receiver rather than for the giver.

Second and Subsequent Observations and Conferences

Mentors and mentees will require more than one observation-and-conference sequence to establish a strong, trusting relationship. Once this level of trust has been achieved, the mentor and the beginning teacher are ready to proceed to other observations and conferences focused on specific instructional growth for the beginning teacher. This process of preconference, observation, and postconference should continue throughout the year, changing focus as the needs of the beginning teacher change. See Box 5.3 for helpful guidelines.

Tools for Observation

Using observation tools is like taking snapshots of classroom events. The purpose is to record, in an objective and usable manner, the verbal and nonverbal behaviors of students and teachers. Many types of observation tools exist; following are some examples. Mentors and their mentees are encouraged to use whatever observation tools and techniques they agree will be helpful or to develop their own.

Seating Charts

Several techniques for observing student and teacher behaviors make use of the seating chart format. These techniques have several advantages:

- They are easy to use and interpret.
- A large body of information can be recorded on a single chart.
- They deal with relatively important aspects of classroom behavior.
- They enable the observer to record one student's behavior while at the same time observing the teacher and the class as a whole.

Box 5.3

Guidelines to Help a Mentee in Subsequent Observations and Conferences

Preobservation Conference (5-10 minutes)
- Set dates and times for observation and postconference.
- Agree upon what is to be observed.
- Determine where the observer is to sit in the class.
- Discuss the lesson plan and material to be taught.
- Specify the observation tools to be used (see next section).

Observation (20-50 minutes)
- Observe one or two teaching behaviors or strategies.
- Use the observation form agreed upon in preconference.

Postobservation Conference (10-30 minutes)
- Set a relaxed tone.
- Discuss objective data, not viewpoints or judgments.
- Explore strategies, alternatives, causes, and effects.
- Discuss areas of focus for future observations and other activities.

1. *Student/Teacher Question Patterns.* A seating chart can be used to record the frequency of each student's interaction with the teacher during a question-and-answer session.

Directions. When the teacher asks an individual student a question, place an arrow in that student's box on the seating chart. The arrow should be pointing away from the teacher. Each subsequent question directed to that student should be marked with a slash through the same arrow. In Figure 5.2, one student was asked two questions, and the other student was asked four questions.

Figure 5.2. Question Patterns: Teacher to Individual Student

When the teacher directs questions to the entire class, place an arrow in or near the teacher's box on the classroom map/seating chart (see Figure 5.3). The arrow should point in the direction of the class. Subsequent questions directed to the entire class should be recorded as slash marks through the same arrow.

When a student asks a question or responds to the teacher's question, place an arrow in or near that student's box on the seating chart (see Figure 5.4). In this instance, the arrow should point toward the teacher. Subsequent questions and responses by the student should be marked by slashes through the same arrow.

2. *On-Task Behavior.* A seating chart or classroom map is useful for providing data on whether students are engaged in appropriate, "on-task" behavior at specified times during a lesson or activity.

Directions. Observe the class at three- or five-minute intervals. Using the agreed-upon behavior categories, note what each student is doing at the specified times, and mark the appropriate symbols in the student's box. In

Figure 5.3. Question Patterns: Teacher to Entire Class

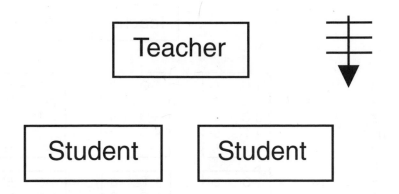

Figure 5.4. Question Patterns: Student to Teacher

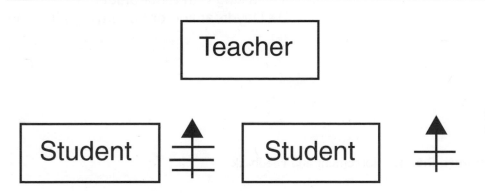

Figure 5.5, two students were chatting with others (i.e., were off task) at 9:00, but all students were on task at 9:03.

3. *Reinforcement and Feedback.* A seating chart may also be used to record teacher responses to individual student behavior. An observer/mentor (with the beginning teacher's agreement) may wish to learn whether the beginning teacher's communications with the class (or with an individual student) are predominantly positive, for example.

Directions. Each time the teacher provides feedback to an individual student, decide whether the feedback is a reprimand, a positive response (such as a compliment or affirmation), a correction, or a neutral response. Then place the symbol for that feedback in the student's box (see Figure 5.6).

Figure 5.5. On-Task Behavior

Teacher

1.	9:00
2.	9:03
3.	9:06
4.	9:09
5.	9:12
6.	9:15
7.	9:18
8.	9:21
9.	9:24
10.	9:27

```
1-O    6-        1-O    6-        1-T    6-
2-O    7-        2-O    7-        2-O    7-
3-O    8-        3-O    8-        3-T    8-
4-T    9-        4-O    9-        4-O    9-
5-    10-        5-    10-        5-    10-

1-O    6-        1-T    6-        1-O    6-
2-O    7-        2-O    7-        2-O    7-
3-O    8-        3-T    8-        3-O    8-
4-O    9-        4-T    9-        4-O    9-
5-    10-        5-    10-        5-    10-
```

Suggested Symbols:
O - On task
T - Talking with other students
D - Daydreaming or not paying attention

Figure 5.6. Reinforcement and Feedback

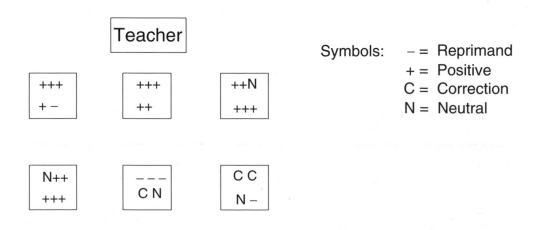

Teacher

Symbols:
− = Reprimand
+ = Positive
C = Correction
N = Neutral

```
+++        +++        ++N
+ −        ++         +++

N++        − − −        C C
+++        C N          N −
```

4. *Classroom Movement Patterns.* The observer/mentor and the beginning teacher may be interested in recording teacher and/or student movement around the classroom during a period of time. Data on a seating chart or classroom map may provide information concerning teacher bias, classroom management procedures, student engagement, or some other aspect of classroom behavior.

Directions. Use lines with arrows to show which students move about the room during the observation period (see Figure 5.7).

Draw lines with arrows to record *teacher* movement during the observation (see Figure 5.8).

Figure 5.7. Student Movement Patterns

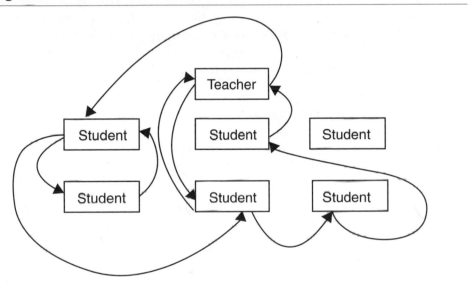

Figure 5.8. Teacher Movement Patterns

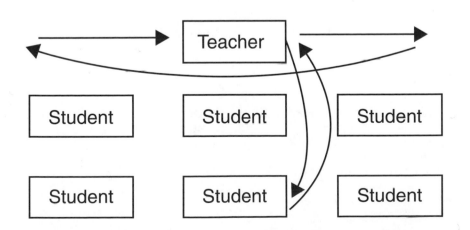

Cause-and-Effect Records

This observation tool is designed to give the observer/mentor and the beginning teacher information concerning the influence of the teacher's actions on student response in the classroom. It can be useful for observing a teacher's classroom management, questioning strategies, direction giving, and other behaviors that call for a student response.

Directions. Divide a blank sheet of paper into two columns. Record teacher actions in the left-hand column and student response to these actions in the right-hand column (see Figure 5.9).

Verbatim Transcripts

Many mentors and supervisors have been trained to use an exact written record of teacher-and-student verbal interactions during an observation period. Whether it is selective (i.e., whether the kinds of verbal events to be recorded have been decided upon beforehand) or a complete account of teacher-and-student verbal behavior, the verbatim transcript allows for a rather thorough analysis of what has transpired in the classroom during

Figure 5.9. Cause-and-Effect Record

Teacher	Student (response)
Bell	Students moving to their seats
Roll taken	Students talking quietly to each other
Surveys class	Room quiets down
Teacher turns on overhead and says, "Take out a piece of paper and answer the following questions about yesterday's reading assignment."	Students look at overhead and some students begin to take out paper

the observation. Many experts advocate the use of the verbatim transcript because of its specificity in providing the beginning teacher with feedback.

Videotapes

Videotaping a lesson for the mentor and the beginning teacher to review together later can also provide valuable information. This is especially helpful if the camera is set up to catch student body language and facial expressions. In this way, both participants can "observe" the lesson together during the feedback cycle.

INFORMAL CONTACT

"I didn't even think of this until we started talking about it today," a first-year teacher in middle school language arts professed to her mentor one day as the two conversed. "Oh, now that makes sense when I hear myself saying it," she said another time. Yet a third time, she exclaimed, "I feel like the sun's come out! I know this is the way we need to go."

—"Kelly," first-year middle school teacher (Stanulis & Weaver, 1998, p. 136)

In their report of the study involving this inexperienced teacher, Stanulis and Weaver (1998) write, "In setting aside the time to talk, we were honoring one of the primary ways in which teachers do business and make meaning: talking about issues and problems with a colleague" (p. 136).

In fact, informal contact, the easiest form of assistance to provide, may also be the most helpful overall. Beginning teachers and mentors frequently state that informal discussions with experienced teachers are the most valuable source of assistance. The beginning teacher needs to know about so many "nuts and bolts"—but doesn't. Even the policies and procedures that *are* explained in preservice orientation often are forgotten in the excitement of the new school year. A bit of information, some timely suggestions, or a few words of understanding and encouragement can be a big help.

Effective mentors make a point of visiting their mentees and generally being around, especially the first few days of school. In fact, when asked to list qualities in a good mentor, one respondent to the survey of San Francisco mentors noted simply "being *available* to the mentee for discussions, exploration, etc." (Jonson, 1999b). Close physical proximity between the mentor's and the mentee's classrooms is highly desirable to facilitate informal contact. This allows the mentor to meet informally but frequently with the beginning teacher to discuss such day-to-day concerns as

- Taking attendance
- Understanding school discipline policies
- Acquiring supplies and materials
- Planning classroom instruction
- Coping with daily problems
- Understanding contracts and benefits

Any concerns of beginning teachers are valid subjects for frequent informal conferences. Consequently, the mentor should make an effort to be both available and easily accessible to the beginning teacher, especially during the first few weeks of the school year.

ASSISTANCE WITH AN ACTION PLAN FOR PROFESSIONAL GROWTH

An important premise of coaching shared by other promising practices is the view of professional growth as ongoing learning. Conditions necessary for the professional growth of teachers parallel essential ingredients of adult development. Educators, like all adult learners, need the autonomy to direct and take responsibility for their own learning. (Levine, 1989, p. 243)

One important key to successful mentoring is moving the mentee from some level of dependence on the mentor-teacher to a high level of self-direction. As a logical step in this process, the mentee can begin to plan, formally or informally, a professional development process. This process is apart from any evaluation of the mentee and can follow the processes of observation, demonstration, coaching, and reflection.

Mentors must be conscious of how their own professional development serves as a model for their mentees. Lifelong learning is as much an attitude as an activity. It is a way of life for professionals.

Many kinds of professional planning assistance are possible. The mentor-teacher can assist in planning professional development by

- Sharing views concerning possible career paths and goals
- Providing direct assistance: answering questions, suggesting strategies, supplying resources
- Creating opportunities for the mentee to become involved in professional activities—such as faculty activities, professional associations, special projects—and to "prove" herself as a professional
- Providing information on the mentor's own professional development plan as a model
- Assisting the mentee in setting short- and long-term professional goals

- Acting as a resource to help the mentee obtain information such as certification and continuing education requirements
- Suggesting or providing books, articles, professional videos, and so on.

Appendix A contains sample forms that a mentor might review with a mentee to help the mentee define goals for growth. These goals should be short-term, achievable within a few months. Plans should be revisited and revised or rewritten two or three times per year so that the beginning teacher can gain a sense of accomplishment and growth.

In addition, the mentor should be sensitive to the beginning teacher's own agenda for professional development. Many beginning teachers are as busy as they can be just filling the requirements of maintaining their credentials. Some work to complete a master's degree in the first year or two while they are working. Any other plans for development should be coordinated with these activities.

ROLE MODELING

The aspect of role modeling is not one I consciously set about doing. But, more than in other areas, mentees tell me in conversations several years later that they wanted to "be like [me]." To me, that is a hidden part of mentoring. But if the mentee doesn't feel that respect and admiration for the mentor, why would he pay attention to the mentor's ideas? I also think the respect other colleagues show for the mentor gives the mentee more reason to want to learn from the mentor.

—A mentor (Jonson, 1999b)

Literature on mentoring emphasizes the importance of providing beginning teachers with role models for personal and professional behavior. What seems to confirm and enhance the mentoring relationship is the mentee's respect for the mentor as a professional and as a human being who is living a life worthy of that respect. In addition to helping the beginning teacher acquire skills and knowledge, the mentor-teacher must model a commitment to professional growth (see Box 5.4). Important to the mentoring relationship is not just what the mentor *knows*, but who he *is*.

Role modeling means much more than demonstration teaching by the mentor. It means exhibiting the mentor's professionalism; it means showing the mentee how to get things done within the political climate of the school; it means demonstrating realistic ways of solving problems; it means exhibiting energy, self-confidence, security, and competency.

Box 5.4

The Mentor-Teacher as a Model

The mentor-teacher becomes a model:
- In relations with colleagues, students, parents, and others
- By demonstrating a commitment to student growth and development
- By demonstrating exemplary skills in the classroom
- In collaborative endeavors with other professionals (collegial interaction and support)
- In work habits
- By modeling a professional growth commitment and having a personal and professional development plan
- By active involvement in professional activities and professional organizations
- By seeking knowledge of trends in education, including new teaching materials, methodology, and research
- By expressing a positive set of values and beliefs concerning teaching as a career
- By being a facilitator of change and improvement

With the aid of an effective role model, the mentee develops a sense of professional identity and competence. The mentor, in turn, profits in the areas of technical and psychological support, internal satisfaction, and increased respect from colleagues (Kram, 1985).

CONCLUSION

This chapter has reviewed the many strategies and tools mentors may use to work with beginning or other new teachers, including information about when to use the strategies and recommended procedures. Chapter 6 looks at general things to keep in mind when working as a partner with an adult learner.

6

Working as a Partner With the Adult Learner

Teaching was the fulfillment of a lifelong dream for Sherie, 40, a first-year elementary school teacher. When Sherie was an intern, her site principal noticed her strong teaching abilities, outgoing personality, and unusual dedication. He took a personal interest in her teaching career, offered her advice during her internship, and encouraged her to stay at his school site during her first official year of teaching.

As the teacher of a first- and second-grade combination class with students from many language backgrounds, Sherie worked diligently at maintaining each learner's ethnic integrity. In Saturday seminars, she participated in learning activities based on the *California Standards for the Teaching Profession* (California Commission on Teacher Credentialing and the California Department of Education, 1997). Sherie used the standards to assess her own teaching, and she developed a classroom-research questionnaire to foster her professional growth: "How can I develop teaching strategies that address different student learning styles?" Over the year, she compiled student work and evidence of her teaching practices into a teaching portfolio (WestEd, 1997).

During her first year of teaching, Sherie had two mentors: her principal and her mentor in the Beginning Educators' Seminars on Teaching (BEST) program. Each held regular conversations with her, observed her teaching, listened to her concerns, and offered advice when she asked for it. They provided different perspectives, two backdrops from which she could view teaching as her chosen profession. Latisha, her BEST mentor, conducted four formal, standards-based observations of Sherie's teaching as it related to her research questions. She offered Sherie emotional support and suggestions for classroom management, curriculum planning, assessment, and educational materials. Latisha helped Sherie understand how to meet state and district curriculum standards while individualizing instruction of her culturally diverse students. She reinforced the BEST seminars' emphasis on the importance of reflective conversations and writing. Sherie completed her first year of teaching with a deeper understanding of school and a greater trust in administration than are usually present in novice teachers.

—*Scherer (1999, pp. 116-117)*

A good teacher of children is not necessarily a good mentor of another teacher. Needed above and beyond expertise in teaching is the ability to facilitate the learning of adults. Good mentors stray from the traditional "authoritarian teacher/supplicant learner" archetype. They work on establishing a collaborative learning partnership with their mentee, grounded in knowledge about adult learning.

Adult learning, or *andragogy,* is rooted in principles delineated by Malcolm Knowles (1980) in *The Modern Practice of Adult Education: From Pedagogy to Andragogy.* Knowles points out that adult learners bring their own history of experience to a learning relationship. They learn best when they are engaged as active partners, not when they serve as passive receivers. A good mentor seldom acts as an authority figure, but more often serves as a facilitator, a "guide on the side" rather than a "sage" on or off a stage. Adult mentees—even those initially unsure of themselves and needing extensive support—require as adults as much self-direction as possible, with involvement in diagnosing, planning, implementing, and evaluating their own learning.

Effective mentors of adult learners understand that their role is one mainly of *facilitation.* In a dynamic facilitative process, a mentor-mentee *learning partnership* evolves over time as the developing teacher becomes more and more comfortable and self-directed. Facilitation involves

- Encouraging the beginning teacher to set his own learning objectives
- Involving the beginning teacher in planning how she will learn
- Encouraging the beginning teacher to use a wide variety of resources to get to his objective
- Helping the beginning teacher to implement and evaluate her learning

Beginning teachers want to be treated as equals to their colleagues. It is extremely important when mentoring to treat the mentee as a partner, an equal in the learning process. "The legitimate recognition that [beginning teachers] should be actively involved as both planners and participants in their own learning continues to have a deservedly important impact on the theory and practice of adult education and, by extension, of adult mentoring," writes Cohen (1995, p. 10). A mentee will not necessarily grow in ability or in desire to improve simply because a mentor has discussed a topic or a goal. Rather, the mentor and mentee need to work through ideas together, both fully participating in the process. Experienced mentors report a "balancing act," in which they carefully adjust their mentoring behaviors so as not to tilt the relationship into either inapt control or unrealistic "hands-off." Adult learning requires time for trial and error, reflection, and self-correction. Effective mentors respect their mentees' singular learning curves. They watch for appropriate timing, keeping in mind that the new, often overwhelmed teacher must be ready to grow from the process before any "teaching" can occur. The mentor, in other words, must present suggestions at a time when the mentee is ready to absorb them.

BELIEFS ABOUT SUPERVISION AND MENTORING

Methods of supervising teachers are changing radically from the methods used in the 1980s, when school administrators observed teachers in their classrooms to see how they were doing. "The pattern of the 1980s—when principals were encouraged to be 'instructional leaders' and teacher evaluation and staff development programs were built on 'effective teaching' research—is being challenged," writes John O'Neil (1993, p. 1). "So is the appropriateness of principals' serving dual roles, supervising teachers in the administrative sense (evaluating their performance, for example) while also trying to help them improve their instruction." As a result, experts say, traditional forms of supervision are being questioned. New avenues to teacher growth are more peer oriented and less likely to fit comfortably under the mantle of supervision.

Whereas supervision in the 1980s was based on the evaluation model, most mentoring today is more closely based on some combination of clinical supervision and cognitive coaching models. A quick summary of these models reveals some of the important differences and provides a background for further discussion.

The Evaluation Model. In the traditional evaluation model, the board of trustees and the state or province initiate an evaluation, and only personnel holding an administrative credential are authorized to evaluate. Districts set up policies and deadlines for evaluation of teachers as a way of meeting contractual requirements and controlling quality. Commonly, an evaluator rates the teacher based on standards developed, negotiated, adopted, and made public. Performance behaviors to be evaluated might include such things as punctuality, willingness to participate in extracurricular and professional activities, personal characteristics, professional attitudes and growth, and so on. The evaluator observes the teacher based on the criteria established by the district and enters ratings on a preprinted form. Copies of the evaluation go to the teacher, to the teacher's personnel file, and to the building principal. Teachers receive ratings such as *outstanding, adequate,* or *needs to improve,* for example (Costa & Garmston, 1994, p. 14).

Clinical Supervision. Under this model, an administrator or another supervisor trained in the techniques of clinical supervision works with the teacher to determine objectives, concepts, techniques, materials, and assessment methods. The supervisor then observes in-class instruction, analyzes the data to determine patterns of behavior and critical incidents of teaching and learning, and confers with the new teacher to share the data. The cycle continues, with more planning to determine future directions for growth (Glatthorn, 1984, pp. 7-8). Clinical supervision "is an intensive process designed to improve instruction by conferring with the teacher on lesson planning, observing the lesson, analyzing the observational data, and giving the teacher feedback about the observation" (Glatthorn, 1984, p. 7).

Cognitive Coaching. In the cognitive coaching model, the new teacher allows herself to be coached by someone who is respected for being helpful and having good leadership qualities. The coach may be a department chair or a peer. Coaching begins on the new teacher's first day on the job and can continue throughout the year. Under this model, the new teacher determines criteria relating to student and teacher behavior for the coach to observe. Such behaviors might include classroom interaction, instruction, student learning, student performance, curriculum adherence, individual student behavior, teacher behavior and skills, and so on. The new teacher lets the mentor-coach know what she would like the coach to look for and what feedback would be helpful. After observation, the coach shares any information collected with the new teacher. The new teacher self-evaluates based on the criteria established in a planning period. The goal is to improve instruction, curriculum, and student learning (Costa & Garmston, 1994, p. 14).

Costa and Garmston (1994) outline the following steps in the cognitive coaching cycle:

1. *The planning conference* (Costa & Garmston, 1994, pp. 18-20). The initial conference is a period for building trust. During this conference, the coach focuses attention on the teacher's goals. As the new teacher dis-

cusses his lessons, he refines his strategies, discovers potential problems, and essentially "rehearses" (mentally works through) his upcoming lesson. He also establishes the parameters for a reflecting conference to follow the observation and sets the agenda for that meeting. The planning conference forces the new teacher to think about his instruction plan and promotes future self-coaching.

2. *Observation of the lesson* (Costa & Garmston, 1994, p. 21). During this step, the coach collects data as requested by the teacher and discussed in the planning conference. The idea is for the new teacher to experiment with his own strategies and techniques, with the coach gathering data.

3. *The reflecting conference* (Costa & Garmston, 1994, pp. 21-22). This follow-up conference, according to Costa and Garmston, is best if delayed somewhat after the observation to allow time for the teacher to reflect and analyze and for the coach to organize data and plan the reflective coaching strategy. To begin this conference, the new teacher shares his impressions of the lesson and specific examples supporting those impressions. He is asked to compare what occurred during the lesson with what was planned. Ideally, the coach helps the teacher draw conclusions regarding relationships between his actions and student outcomes. Finally, the new teacher is encouraged to project how new insights will affect future lessons and also to reflect on the coaching process itself.

The Mentor. The traditional mentoring role, then, is based on the model of clinical supervision, with mentoring strategies often following the model of cognitive coaching. The mentee takes an active role, suggesting topics to be addressed; the mentor observes and collects data; and the two meet to reflect, learn, and grow. This formal process can greatly enhance a teacher's ability to apply what is learned to the classroom. According to researchers Joyce and Showers (Albert, Blondino, & McGrath, 1990), in fact, beginning teachers are most likely to use what they know if coaching is built into the staff development process (see Table 6.1).

PHASES IN THE MENTORING RELATIONSHIP: THREE MODELS

The core of mentoring . . . is the focus on collaborative participation and mutual critical thinking and reflection about the process, value, and results of jointly derived learning goals established for the mentee.

—Norman H. Cohen (1995, p. 14)

Mentors and their mentees go through predictable phases in their relationship as it develops and matures over time. Where they are in these phases will determine strategies to be used by the mentor. Cohen (1995, pp. 15-16) summarizes the following four phases:

Table 6.1   Effectiveness of Training Components

	Knowledge	Workshop Application	Classroom Use
Theory	100%	5%	5%
Theory plus demonstration	100%	5%	5%
Theory, demonstration, and practice with feedback	100%	85-90%	5-10%
Theory, demonstration, and practice with feedback and coaching	100%	85-90%	75-85%

SOURCE: From the research of Joyce & Showers, as cited in Albert, Blondino, & McGrath, 1990.

1.   *The early phase.* In the beginning, the mentor-mentee pair focus primarily on building a trusting relationship. The mentee must feel comfortable with the mentor and trust that she will not be judged when she seeks help.

2.   *The middle phase.* Once the mentee is comfortable, the partners exchange information. The mentor accumulates knowledge about the mentee in an effort to understand the mentee's goals and concerns.

3.   *The later phase.* The mentor explores the interests and beliefs of the mentee and attempts to learn the reasons for the mentee's decisions. This might include inviting the mentee to self-appraise.

4.   *The last phase.* The mentor motivates the mentee to reflect on her goals, to pursue challenges, and to follow through on her own personal, educational, and career path.

How quickly a mentee is ready to move from one of these phases to the next varies considerably, depending on the individual. A perceptive mentor will be aware of the mentee's readiness to move on and will let that readiness guide the progression of the relationship.

The Association for Supervision and Curriculum Development (ASCD, 1999a) presents a different model of mentee learning, also breaking the mentor-mentee relationship into four phases. Like Cohen, ASCD's (1999a) *Mentoring to Improve Schools* emphasizes the need for the mentor to be aware of the mentee's progression and to time interventions accordingly. "Be a good listener and ask questions to continually assess the developmental needs of the protégé, the state of mentoring, and the most appropriate mentoring response," ASCD advises.

The four phases of this model (ASCD, 1999a, pp. 103, 105) are the following:

1.   In the beginning, the mentor and mentee start to develop their relationship, with the mentor taking primary responsibility for leadership. The new teacher is just beginning her career and may well drop quickly from excited anticipation of her job into a period of stress and survival. She is most likely to ask basic questions with only one correct answer (e.g., "How do I let the office know how many kids are absent?"). In the beginning, the mentor provides information as needed, then moves on to help the mentee set priorities and direction and to model for the mentee (e.g., how to conduct a class meeting, prepare for a parent conference, or set up a grade book).

2.   Later, the mentee and mentor build a partnership. Often the new teacher by this time is disillusioned with his job and questions the way things are (e.g., "Help! Got any ideas for dealing with this unruly student behavior?") The mentor offers assistance (e.g., providing samples of classroom discipline policies) but at the same time seeks suggestions from the mentee. She attempts to let the mentee take more responsibility for the relationship.

3.   As the mentor-mentee relationship becomes strong, the two enjoy working together, sharing ideas, analyzing, and making decisions together (e.g., "Why do we have so many assemblies? It's hard to get the kids focused back on classwork afterward. I'm losing too much valuable class time!"). The mentor helps with prioritizing but defers to the mentee's judgment whenever possible. The mentee is in a period of rejuvenation.

4.   The mentor begins to withdraw from the relationship, encouraging the mentee to become independent. The *mentor* now uses questions to encourage analysis and reflection from the mentee (e.g., asks the new teacher how a new strategy might affect her students' learning; listens as the new teacher discusses her assessment of examples of student work; engages the new teacher in a reflective conversation about an issue or concern). The mentor defers to the mentee's judgment and affirms the mentee's abilities and understanding. By this time, the mentee is often headed back into a period of anticipation and is ready for self-growth (see Figure 6.1).

Figure 6.1. Dynamics Within the Mentoring Process

The Process of the Protégé's Development

The Protégé's Need for Support Encouragement, and Affirmation / A Protégé's Emotional Level	Anticipation — Survival — Disillusionment — Reflection — Rejuvenation — Anticipation
The Mentoring Styles and Process	Direct → Explain → Share → Delegate
Shifting Leadership Responsibilities in the Mentor-Protégé Relationship	Mentor responsibility for task success / Protégé responsibility for task success
The Strength of the Mentor-Protégé Partnership	Create — Build — Enjoy — Withdraw

SOURCE: Association for Supervision and Curriculum Development (1999a, p. 105).

Joyce and Showers (1982, 1983) and Showers (1985) characterize the process of coaching or mentoring as a similar phased-in approach. They describe five functions:

1. *Providing companionship.* The first function of mentoring is to "provide interchange with another human being over a difficult process" (Joyce & Showers, 1983, p. 19). The mentoring relationship involves mutual reflection, the checking of perceptions, the sharing of frustrations and successes, and the informal thinking through of problems. When one person watches another try a new model of teaching for the first time, for instance, the two will find much to talk about. Companionship provides reassurance that problems are normal. It not only makes the new teacher's learning process technically easier but also enhances the quality of the experience. "It is more pleasurable to share a new thing than to do it in isolation. The lonely business of teaching has sorely lacked the companionship that we envision for our coaching teams" (Joyce & Showers, 1983, p. 19). Companionship also helps overcome the tendency to avoid the awkwardness of practicing a new strategy.

2. *Giving technical feedback.* In the course of their relationship, the team will reach the stage where the mentor will provide feedback on observations of the mentee's teaching. This technical feedback is not to be confused with general evaluation. Feedback does not imply judgment about the overall quality of teaching but is confined to information about the execution of specific skills. The mentor might point out omissions, examine how materials are arranged, check to see whether all parts of a teaching strategy have been brought together, and so on. Technical feedback keeps the mind of the developing teacher on the business of perfecting skills, polishing them, and working through problem areas. Whether the mentee is trying a new model of teaching, implementing a new curriculum, or setting up a classroom management system, feedback must be accurate, specific, and nonjudgmental.

3. *Analyzing application and extending executive control.* As the new teacher's skills develop and solidify, mentoring moves into a more complex stage: mutual examination of appropriate use of new strategies:

> The cognitive aspects of transferring new behaviors into effective classroom practice are more difficult than the interactive moves of teaching. While all teachers can develop skill in performing a new teaching strategy fairly readily, the harder tasks come as the skill is applied in the classroom. (Showers, 1985, p. 14)

One of the important things a new teacher learns is when to use a new model appropriately and what will be achieved by doing so. Selecting the right occasions to use a teaching strategy is not as easy as it sounds. For instance, the new teacher may have learned in college about inductive teaching strategies, such as concept attainment, and may have had little difficulty learning the pattern of the models and discussing the models with materials provided. But it is a different task to select concepts to teach in his own classroom, reorganize materials from the standard textbook, teach students to respond to the new strategy, and create lessons he has never seen demonstrated directly. In this phase, these tasks become the substance of conversations between the new and the experienced teachers. The new teacher is developing what Joyce and Showers (1982, 1983) call *executive control*—that is, a "meta understanding" about how the strategy works, how it can be fitted into the instructional repertoire, and how to modify or create instructional materials for its use. "Executive control" comes with the new teacher's growing judgment and competence.

4. *Adapting to the students.* A new teacher expends much energy trying to figure out how best to apply new teaching strategies to his particular group of students. Successful teaching means that students are responding successfully. Mentors can help new teachers adapt strategies to fit the needs of their students and can suggest ways of acquainting students with what is expected of them:

One of the major functions of the coach is to help [the mentee] to "read" the responses of the students to make decisions about skill training and how to adapt the model. This is especially important in the early stages of practice when teachers are concerned with their own behavior and it is difficult to worry about the students as well. (Joyce & Showers, 1982, p. 7)

5. *Facilitating.* Successfully implementing any new teaching method requires *practice.* Mentors should expect that a new teacher's early tries will not come close to reaching standards. With this in mind, Joyce and Showers (1982) point out, a major job of mentors is to help their mentees feel good about themselves during these early trials. "Teachers' lack of interpersonal support and close contact with others in the context of teaching is a tragedy. Coaching reduces this isolation and increases support" (p. 7).

In his book *Mentor: Guiding the Journey of Adult Learners,* Laurent Daloz (1999) explains facilitation this way:

It is very important to watch for the growing edge, like a coach photographing their forward movement and replaying it for them. This may mean being very explicit about what [mentees] have done well. It is generally more effective to show people when they are on track than to tell them where they should go or to criticize when they have strayed. *Emphasize positive movement*, underline it, restate it, praise it. By spending undue time on the negative, we run the risk of helping our [mentees] construct a vision of the impossible, whereas our job is to help them imagine the possible and then move toward it. Always we are guides, encouraging movement. (pp. 123-124)

All three of these mentoring models move along a continuum to a more facilitative approach. The goal is autonomy for the beginning teacher to self-assess and self-prescribe. The mentor assumes different support and assessment roles at different stages of the continuum of the relationship. In the early stages, information tends to flow from mentor to the beginning teacher, with the mentor offering suggestions and solutions. As the beginning teacher develops increasing autonomy, the relationship becomes more collaborative, with the beginning teacher and the mentor reflecting and co-constructing solutions.

GETTING TO TRUST

Trust: assured reliance on the character, ability, strength, or truth of someone or something.

—*Merriam Webster's Collegiate Dictionary,* 10th ed.

In each of the mentoring sequences just described, the pattern of an evolving relationship is built on a foundation of trust. Feelings of jitteriness, tension, fear, and nervousness have no place in the relationship. Trust is a vital aspect of school life that influences basic patterns of interpersonal and group behavior. From the beginning, mentors need to establish trust between themselves and the new teachers they work with. Trust is a fundamental feature of mentoring and pervades all successful mentor-protégé relationships (see Box 6.1). As one San Francisco mentor put it, "You must get to trust, or you get nowhere."

To establish trust, a mentor must demonstrate openness, honesty, and candor. Such openness breeds confidence and trust: A person who seeks to conceal nothing, in all likelihood, does not seek to harm others. Effective mentors are willing to be treated as human beings and do not tend to hide behind the cloak of bureaucratic power and seniority. Such candor and authenticity promote a climate of trust and intimacy. In a trusting relationship, the beginning teacher believes that she can depend on the mentor in difficult situations, that she can rely on the integrity of this new colleague, and that confidentiality will not be broken. In contrast, a mentor displaying inauthentic behavior has been characterized as "playing the role," "manipulating and using people and the system," "passing the buck," and "blaming others for his own mistakes and shortfalls." See Box 6.2 for a list of ways to build trust.

Strange as it may sound, simply listening—with concern—is one of the best ways to build trust. "Just listening" can build a relationship. This is difficult for many mentors who understand the myriad tasks confronting their new teachers and want very much to tell them what works, to analyze, to question, to support. Often the new teacher needs encouragement, but in many cases this kind of help is not helpful at all.

"As a mentor project, I have held meetings for the new teachers at my school," one San Francisco mentor says (Jonson, 1999b). "Partly we focus on school activities such as an all-school writing test, but mostly the meetings are open-ended so the teachers can bring concerns and questions as well as stories of successes."

Box 6.1

Trust

- Trust is built by focusing directly on it.
- Taking risks is necessary to build trust.
- Getting supported for taking risks builds trust.
- Allowing yourself to be vulnerable increases others' trust of you.
- Caring about each other is necessary to establish trust.
- Letting go of negative incidents in the past is critical to trust building.

Box 6.2

A Menu of Trust Builders

- Ensure—and keep—confidentiality.
- Hold regular team meetings, with both task and trust issues on the agenda.
- Clarify expectations.
- Discuss expectations.
- Negotiate expectations.
- Be congruent. Walk the talk.
- Create multidirectional communications.
- Respect, honor, and celebrate each individual's style.
- Confront directly with caring.
- Focus on gains, not losses.
- Describe, don't evaluate.
- Delegate power and authority.
- Admit your own mistakes and vulnerability.
- Be a risk taker when it comes to trusting others.
- Create interactions.
- Share feelings as well as thoughts.
- Accept that we all get frustrated and angry at times.
- Encourage balance and renewal for the team and for each individual.
- Celebrate—even mistakes.
- Practice openness.
- Play, laugh, use humor with love and respect.
- Listen actively.

Ineffective mentors often have one or two styles of responses for most situations. Following are some typical ways of responding to problems.

Judging. The mentor might judge the mentee's thoughts or behaviors in some way. This judgment might be favorable (e.g., "That's a good idea," "You're on the right track now") or unfavorable ("An attitude like that won't get you anywhere"). In either case, the implication is that the mentor is superior and can pass judgment on the speaker's thoughts or actions. Furthermore, judgmental language is likely to make the beginning teacher defensive. This type of response might put the beginning teacher on guard and, in so doing, end the conversation and the possibility of help. "My mentee and I have a trusting relationship in that he can be open and honest when he needs to," one San Francisco mentor says. "He does not fear my judgment." (On the other hand, a mentor *can* help the beginning teacher evaluate and reflect on a situation in a nonjudgmental way.)

Analyzing. The analyzer's response suggests that he understands the mentee better than the mentee understands himself: "What's bothering you is . . ." or "What you really think is . . ." Two problems are associated with this sort of analyzing. First, the mentor's interpretation may not be correct, in which case the new teacher may become even more confused by accepting it. Second, even if the mentor's analysis is accurate, sharing it might not be useful to the mentee. It may make the mentee defensive (because analyzing implies superiority), or the beginning teacher may not be able to understand the mentor's view of the problem. Analyzing can be a way to help a beginning teacher see the "blind parts" of himself or a situation, but many mentors use this style of response too often and too early.

Questioning. Although questioning often helps mentors understand the unclear parts of a mentee's statements, it can also be used to direct the beginning teacher's thoughts. All beginning teachers have likely had the experience of being questioned by a parent, a teacher, or another authority figure who seemed to be trying to trap them. Used in this way, questioning implies that the person doing the asking already has some idea of what direction the discussion should take. The careful mentor will instead choose open-ended questions and will avoid questions that begin with "Why?"

Supporting. Sometimes the beginning teacher just needs encouragement, and a supporting response is the best thing in these cases. In many cases, however, this kind of response is not really much help. Telling an obviously upset beginning teacher that "everything is all right" or joking about a problem can communicate that the mentor does not accept the mentee's feelings or that the mentee's feelings are not justified.

Good intentions are not always enough. All of these responses may be helpful at times, but they often confuse the person asking for help, making him feel defensive or worse than before he shared his problem. The mentor may be right about what caused the mentee's problem and how the mentee could solve the problem, but if the beginning teacher does not discover the answer for himself, it may not be useful to him. As one overzealous mentor commented, "[My mentee] often ignores the truth, even when it's so obvious you'd think she would trip over it."

Fortunately, another way of responding can often be much more helpful. This style of response is simply *active listening.* With active listening, the mentor maintains eye contact, asks questions to clarify, and otherwise helps the beginning teacher to clarify. The mentor paraphrases the beginning teacher's statements to check her understanding of what she hears, usually beginning by saying something like, "What I hear you telling me is . . ." In these kinds of conversations, it is important that the mentor feed back only what she has heard the beginning teacher say without making any judgment or offering an interpretation. In building trust, the mentor's job is simply to *understand*, not to analyze or judge. Also, the mentor should use her own language in checking back with the beginning teacher rather than just parrot the original words.

To understand how listening can be so worthwhile, mentors need to realize that their role is really not to solve all their mentees' problems for them. Mentors can, however, help beginning teachers work things out for themselves. This is a difficult lesson for many mentors to learn. When someone they care for and are charged with supporting is in trouble and feeling bad, their first tendency is to try to make things better—to answer questions, soothe hurts, fix whatever is bothersome. Even in cases when the mentor is sure she knows what is right for the person, however, it is generally necessary to let that person discover the solution for himself. Active listening is easy to implement, but its importance cannot be overemphasized in the development of mentor-mentee trust.

ADULT LIVES, ADULT LEARNING STYLES

> I need to understand Jean's whole life; I need to be able to see all the pressures on her. . . . I think we can work with the whole framework, the holistic approach, so that the chances of success are going to be greater than if we don't focus on the whole picture of the adult.
>
> —Laurent A. Daloz (1999, p. 110)

As mentors work with beginning teachers, they must keep in mind the whole of the beginning teacher's life. The temptation to "steer them into courses you know would be good for them without regard for their capacity to handle the work, given the rest of the forces in their lives" (Daloz, 1999, p. 110) is often great. Many of these beginning teachers are caught between duties at home/family relationships and the responsibilities of school/students' needs. They struggle to define new personal and professional lives. They are "learning to swim" in the give-and-take of whirling new roles. "It's a journey with a lot of potholes and trees across the road, and thunderstorms, and needing to take detours," one mentor explains. "Last term she really had to take a detour, and maybe she's had to fill in a couple of potholes this year, but she's underway again, still moving ahead" (Daloz, 1999, p. 109).

So what's a mentor to do? When facing difficult real-life challenges with her mentee, one mentor responded,

> Maybe just trying to be there with the flashlight and keeping the door at various places of the journey open when she wants or feels that she is able to make it in . . . helping her find balance, looking at the different piles of stuff in her life with the old flashlight and

saying, "Where are you going to put this chunk called school?" (Daloz, 1999, p. 109)

Mentors must see themselves as facilitators of learning, all the while "listening, empowering, coaching, challenging, teaching, collaborating, aiding, assisting, supporting, expediting, easing, simplifying, advancing, and encouraging" (Zachary, 2000, p. 23). "Facilitators of learning see themselves as resources for learning rather than didactic instructors who have all the answers" (Brookfield, 1986, p. 63).

According to Brookfield (1986), "One important element in facilitating adult learning is helping learners become aware of their own idiosyncratic learning styles" (p. 64). Just as children have different learning preferences, patterns, or styles, so do adults. For some, learning through verbal modes is an easy and efficient method. These mentees learn best through their ears, picking up ideas more completely when they get or work with them auditorily. Others seem to grasp ideas more easily if they can see a diagram or a visual representation of what is being discussed. They are at their best when input comes through their eyes. For some, touch is especially important in their thinking and learning. Still others are kinesthetic learners and thinkers; motion and action are significant factors in how they interface with ideas. One mentor described her frustration working with a new teacher until the two of them began their conferences on the middle school playfield. Several times each week, they met on the playfield for a brisk walk around and around, with the young man pouring out his concerns as they pounded the track side by side. Only when the mentee was moving could he really express himself. Just as a child, then, so might the adult mentee benefit from learning strategies that take into account adult learning styles. Knowledge of these different learning styles, as well as of supervision models and stages in teacher development, can help the mentor be more effective in her efforts.

Honoring specific learning styles helps facilitate learning. In her book *The Mentor's Guide: Facilitating Effective Learning Relationships*, Lois Zachary (2000) offers further general guidelines that relate to adult learning styles or patterns of preferred responses.

- *Pace the learning.* The pace of learning varies and is often interrupted by individual need. Sometimes learners withdraw or become avoidant when they are uncomfortable. This self-declared time-out is part of the learning process as well and needs to be acknowledged.
- *Time the developmental intervention.* Mentors need to understand where their mentees are developmentally. They cannot assume readiness.
- *Keep the focus on learning.* Mentoring is not a chemistry contest. The partners should not get hung up on personality issues. Stick with the main attraction: learning.

- *Build the relationship first.* The learning will follow. Too often, mentors and mentees do not make the time to create the appropriate climate for learning.
- *Structure the process.* Sharing the responsibility for structuring the learning relationship (even in an informal learning relationship) improves the quality of the interaction. (Zachary, 2000, pp. 24-25)

In addition, it is always important that the mentor and mentee celebrate successes if the mentee is to remain engaged and enthusiastic. Success invites more success.

THE IMPORTANCE OF REFLECTION

Reflection is the fulcrum of learning that lasts. Without it, I doubt if protégés could sustain the changes we attempt to implement. Reflection provides distance so a protégé can look back at what has happened. The word *reflection* brings a mirror to mind. When we hold up a mirror, we can examine images in detail. Without it, we could have a distorted view or no view at all.

—Jane Fraser (1998, p. 55)

Whether it's student behavior or student writing, classroom relationships or classroom logistics, information from parents or information from administrators, the many issues that a teacher deals with throughout the day provide plenty of substance for reflection. To reflect, as *Merriam Webster's Collegiate Dictionary* (10th ed.) defines it, is "to think seriously; contemplate; ponder." Without such reflection, past events and occurrences disappear into history. Whether they have been dealt with well or not, they are done. With reflection upon past events, though, they become stepping-stones to improvement, opportunities for growth. When a teacher thinks about what he has learned from an experience, he can consolidate his knowledge and skills, evaluate his own performance, recognize successes, and develop strategies for improvement. For these reasons, reflecting on specific teaching problems as well as on larger professional and career development issues is important.

"In teaching, as in life, maximizing meaning from experiences requires reflection," write Costa and Kallick (2000).

The act of reflection, particularly with a group of teaching colleagues, provides an opportunity for

- amplifying the meaning of one's work through the insights of others;
- applying meaning beyond the situation in which it was learned;

- making a commitment to modifications, plans, and experimentation; and

- documenting learning and providing a rich base of shared knowledge. (Costa & Kallick, 2000, p. 60)

While reflection may seem to be a natural process, however, in fact, it is not. In a study of 42 preservice teachers at a midwestern university, researchers found that those who received specific training in reflecting had significantly higher levels of reflection than did those in a control group. Notably, some who did not receive training improved their reflection skills anyway through repeated reflective exercises (Galvez-Martin, Bowman, & Morrison, 1999, p. 4). This study illustrates the need to work on the skill of reflection and to practice reflection regularly to realize its benefits.

Reflecting is at its most powerful when teachers collaborate in an active, honest search for answers. Perhaps the best way to reflect—the most productive—is *out loud,* talking with a mentor or a peer. Mentoring, in fact, is really just one teacher facilitating the growth of another. An active listener can be an important source of information for a beginning teacher, can provide emotional support, and often helps the beginning teacher to grow and gain strength as a professional. Reflection should be a part of many of the teaching strategies discussed in Chapter 5: notably, demonstration teaching, observation and feedback, informal contact, and assistance with an action plan for professional growth.

Following interviews with 22 mentor-teachers in southern California, Shulman and Colbert reported that the mentors "suggested that teaching teachers how to reflect on their own teaching is what mentoring should ultimately include, because it will engender teachers with a mode for lifelong improvement and revitalization" (Shulman & Colbert, 1988, p. 9).

Life can only be understood backwards; but it must be lived forwards.

—Søren Kierkegaard (quoted in Costa & Kallick, 2000, p. 60)

CONCLUSION

A teacher talented in working with children may not necessarily have the skills to work well with teachers as adults. This chapter reviewed different aspects of working with adult teachers: models of supervision used through the years, models of teacher development, the need to build a trusting relationship, adult learning styles, and the importance of reflection in adult learning.

Chapter 7 steps back to ask the questions, Why be a mentor? What are the pitfalls, and what are the payoffs?

I needed these two years of support, having the time to deal with problems and being able to see myself in the "stages of development" for a beginning teacher as I ride the roller coaster through the depths of despair in December and January and then go back uphill toward the end of the year.

—Cathy, a beginning teacher ("Teacher Voices," 1996, p. 3)

7

Why Be a Mentor?
The Pitfalls and Payoffs

I love working with new teachers. I love working with enthusiastic and dedicated people. I learn from them and try to make them see that teaching is a learning process. I feel that, as a mentor, I am helping new teachers adjust to the rigorous life of a teacher, yet understand their importance in a child's life. I'm preparing them so that I can retire feeling that I'm leaving our schools in safe hands. Working with new teachers makes me have faith in the future of public education—most of them are great teachers!

—*A mentor (Jonson, 1999b)*

If teachers in general are dedicated educators, mentors are optimally so. Not only are they competent teachers, but they are teachers who willingly extend themselves, continually helping others while seeking professional growth and personal rejuvenation.

A now-classic synthesis of the research on mentoring beginning teachers (Gray & Gray, 1985) revealed that exemplary mentors

- Are secure
- Have power and expertise
- Are goal oriented
- Like and trust their mentees

- Take a personal interest in the careers of their mentees
- Encourage their mentees for their ideas
- Help their mentees to gain confidence and become self-directed professionals

The decision to accept a mentorship role can lead to one of the most professionally rewarding experiences of a teacher's career. No matter how competent the individual teacher and how great the motivation, however, mentoring is ultimately a lot of work, requiring both time and commitment beyond the already-significant time and commitment required of a teacher. If the mentor becomes caught up in one or more of several potential pitfalls associated with the position, the decision to serve as a mentor can lead to considerable frustration.

What are some of these potential pitfalls? And why would a teacher take the position anyway? The pitfalls can be serious, but those who avoid them will find plenty of payoffs.

THE PITFALLS

Unless a protégé is explicit in the discussion of her learning, a mentor cannot always be sure what new ideas are being assimilated. I may come to the end of a mentoring relationship and be unclear about what has been accomplished. But I have learned that some ideas will not be absorbed until a future time. I may need to be satisfied with little things, such as a comment, a smile, a willingness to learn. (Fraser, 1998, p. 51)

There are times when a mentor may not be sure of what she is accomplishing, of whether her long hours and exhausting efforts are bearing results. This is certainly one of the intangible, sometimes frustrating, aspects of the responsibility, countering the many times when a mentor can clearly see the results of her input. It is only one of many potential pitfalls, however. Behaviors associated with other pitfalls—some of which can be guarded against—fall into roughly four categories:

1. Overextending

2. Proceeding without clarification of the mentor's role and without training and support
   a. From the administration
   b. From the mentee

3. Assuming too much responsibility for the mentee

4. Underutilizing professional growth

Overextending

Teachers want to be effective managers of their personal and professional lives. Often, though, because of their professional commitment, they find themselves saying yes to too many projects. Many teachers have "caretaker personalities." They care for and give to others much more than they take care of themselves. They might join a text adoption committee or a curriculum planning team, for example, or they might supervise a student group—or serve as a mentor. Unfortunately, some believe in the myth of a Super Teacher, a teacher who can do all that is asked of him—and do it perfectly. Mentors need not try to be superhuman; they need simply to strive and to care.

In a survey of five mentors for new teachers (four high school and one elementary) in Marin County, California, mentors were asked about their experiences and insights regarding effective mentoring (Smith, 1993, p. 10). All five were glad to be mentors (p. 16), they said, but they discussed "nonsuccesses" in their efforts as well as "successes." All of these mentors felt that they were spread too thin, that they didn't have enough time to do all they wanted to do, and that funds for accomplishing goals were sparse (p. 13).

Some mentoring programs are set up to avoid these problems, with mentors released from some of their other teaching responsibilities or with retired teachers hired to serve as mentors. In other programs, however, mentors are expected to combine their responsibilities as a mentor with their responsibilities of full-time teaching. In these cases, the mentor needs to learn to choose a limited number of activities carefully and then simply to say a professional no to other extra duties or committees. Teachers need to set realistic goals and standards and to focus on celebrating successes. They must learn to replenish and to receive in balance with their giving.

Proceeding Without Clarification of the Mentor's Role

Of the five Marin County mentors surveyed, three expressed "a sense of confusion and anxiety because they were unclear what their jobs were and who they were accountable to" (Smith, 1993, p. 13). Clarification of the role can come through training, through working with a mentor coordinator, and through ongoing communication. Mentors need to establish guidelines both with the administration and with the mentees themselves.

The Administration. Potential mentors should investigate building and district commitment to the program in terms of policy and procedure statements, budgetary allocations, and processes necessary to ensure the ongoing success of the project. Establishing clearly defined expectations between mentors and administrators is absolutely necessary. Consistent feedback and communication between these groups are also necessary, as is follow-up support.

"Remember to inform your principal of your plans," one experienced mentor advises (Jonson, 1999b). "List some ideas, activities, and other pertinent information you need to share with your principal." Supportive resources—such as additional planning time, materials, and technical assistance—do not magically appear at the onset of a mentor-teacher program. These types of continuing support, all too often absent, however, are crucial. "While training usually occurs before mentors take up their new responsibilities," writes Feiman-Nemser (1996), "mentors are more likely to develop their practice as mentors if they also have opportunities to discuss questions and problems that arise in the course of the work with novices" (p. 3).

Marin County mentors also expressed wariness about administrators who attempted to "make gray [the] line" between mentoring and evaluating; all agreed that they should not evaluate their mentees despite their administrators' wishes (Smith, 1993, pp. 13-14). In addition, all five of these mentors noted that other faculty members sometimes had negative feelings toward mentors. "I know there's all these hard feelings [that I got the job and others didn't]," one said. Mentor support groups might help combat this problem, one suggested.

The Mentee. A beginning teacher may not clearly understand what to expect from the mentor. Is the mentor an arm of the administration? Will the mentor make unreasonable demands on the mentee's time? Can the mentor be trusted with professional concerns? Again, it is best to keep mentoring entirely separate from the teacher evaluation process and to reinforce this issue consistently with the beginning teacher.

In the Marin County survey, some of the mentors addressed nonsuccesses directly related to the mentees themselves. Mentors felt frustrated that the mentees were not always willing to take advantage of what was offered to them. One mentor called a meeting of new teachers in her district but was dismayed when only four came. "People said, well, I got your letter and I didn't have time to open it and it's still in my pile. . . . Or, I was going to come but I had to do this instead," the mentor reported (quoted in Smith, 1993, p. 12). All five of the mentors recognized that the new teachers were simply overwhelmed by their jobs (p. 12). One mentor also pointed out that mentees sometimes worried that others would see them as incompetent if they asked for help from a mentor (p. 13).

The mentor and the beginning teacher, then, must work together to establish the parameters of the mentor's responsibilities and expectations. One way to do this is by setting up an action plan (see Appendix A). Working together on such a plan allows both parties to address their needs and concerns and helps them feel comfortable within their respective roles.

Assuming Too Much Responsibility for the Mentee

Mentors may become overly involved with the beginning teacher, fostering a relationship of dependency. The mentor commonly is overprotective or assumes too many obligations to ensure the mentee's success. It is of paramount importance that mentors have a clearly defined concept of facilitating as compared to defending.

Mentors may face the unwelcome reality that a beginning teacher has significant deficiencies or problems beyond the mentor's ability or authority to address. Many mentors, for instance, feel they have an ethical obligation to report problems when a mentee's actions are harmful to the students in her care. The best approach to such issues will often depend on existing building policies and procedures. A decision to break confidentiality and seek assistance should not be viewed as failure on the part of the mentor, but more as a professional responsibility—one to be handled prudently and with sensitivity.

Underutilizing Professional Growth

One major misconception is that teaching is relatively simple and easy to learn. In the psychological and developmental literature, however, it is widely recognized that novices do not learn simply by copying or modeling what experts do. Instead, professional growth in teaching has an emerging quality and takes a substantial amount of time. Furthermore, complex understandings and skills follow developmental patterns similar to those of other complex learning endeavors.

To assist beginning teachers in their route from novice to expert, the mentor must not only understand these precepts but also be able to facilitate the beginner's professional growth through a variety of methods and techniques. Mentors must incorporate into their professional repertoire various skills, including working with adult learners, conducting observations and data collections, problem solving, demonstrating empathy, and providing constructive criticism. It is incumbent that mentors take advantage of professional growth opportunities not only to enrich themselves but also to better enable their mentees' growth.

Any effective mentoring program incorporates training components for both mentors and beginning teachers. Unfortunately, because of poor communications, lack of program support, or various other reasons, teachers participating in district-sponsored mentoring programs sometimes find that obtaining release for training is confusing and difficult at best. Essential opportunities and resources are not always available. Again, mentors need to communicate with administrators and clarify specific details and procedures for the program prior to assuming the mentor role.

Table 7.1   Incentives for Staff-Development Accomplishments

Extrinsic Rewards	*Intrinsic Rewards*
Salary increase	Recognition as a role model
Promotion	Appointment as a committee chair
A reduced teaching load for one year	Recognition in a newspaper or some other form of media
Added fringe benefits	Recognition from the school board
Release time	Professional development (with an allowance provided)
Extra planning time	Extra classroom materials
Travel to paid professional meetings	Compliments for a job well done
Continuing education units	Recognition at a school board dinner
Tickets to cultural activities	A credential of appreciation
Magazine subscriptions for the teacher's classroom	Presentation at a professional meeting
	A lunch
	Advancement on a career ladder

SOURCE: Orlich (1989, pp. 77-78).

Figure 7.1. The Payoffs

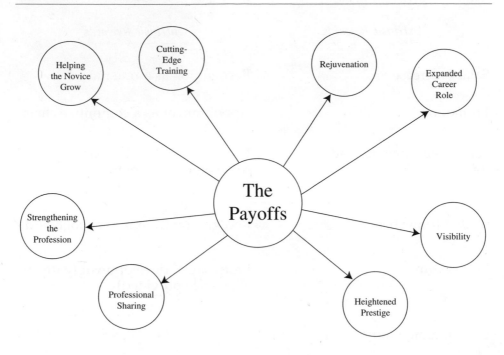

In a study of 158 mentors of student teachers from the University of California, Irvine, mentors filled out questionnaires regarding the benefits they saw from working with mentees beginning in 1991 (Clinard & Ariav, 1998). Although the mentees in this study were student teachers, the issues explored are relevant to any mentor working with a beginning teacher. Researchers were interested in learning the following:

1. What benefits do mentors gain from working with student teachers?

2. Is the mentoring experience having any effect on the mentors' practice (with their students)?

3. Is the mentoring experience having any effect on the mentors beyond the classroom (as professionals and as private individuals)?

Participants ranked benefits in each of these three categories after working with their mentees. See Tables 7.2, 7.3, and 7.4 for their responses.

Ultimately, as Bruce Joyce and Beverly Showers (1995) suggest, a powerful incentive for any staff development activity is simply "the clear understanding that it produces success" (Orlich, 1989, p. 74). And although collegial relationships among teachers are valuable in general,

(text continues on page 128)

Table 7.2   Benefits Gained From Working With Student Teachers

Benefits	UCI Mentors	
	Average[a]	Rank
Enthusiasm	3.50	1
Opportunity to collaborate	3.34	2
Knowledge of subject matter	2.93	3
Reflective mirror	2.90	4
Innovative strategies for teaching	2.90	4
Technology expertise	2.76	5
Insights about individual students' background	2.54	6
Assessment strategies	2.34	7
Sheltered language insights	1.68	8
Bilingual skills and strategies	1.20	9
Working with mainstreamed students	—	—

SOURCE: Clinard & Ariav (1998, p. 10, table 1).

a. Note: Scale in questionnaire was from 0 ("very little contribution") to 4 ("great contribution"). N:89 (out of 158 participating mentors).

Table 7.3   Impact of Coaching Experience on Mentors' Work
in Their Own Classrooms

Practice Areas	UCI Mentors	
	Average[a]	Rank
Reflecting more often on planning and implementation	3.02	1
Using Cognitive Coaching techniques with students in the classroom	2.56	2
Reassessing classroom management and discipline strategies	2.56	2
Using instructional technology more frequently and effectively	2.44	3
Collaborating more with other teachers	2.27	4

SOURCE: Clinard & Ariav (1998, p. 13, table 2).

a. Note: Scale in questionnaire was from 0 ("very little contribution") to 4 ("great contribution"). N:89 (out of 158 participating mentors).

Table 7.4   Impact of the Coaching Experience Beyond the Classroom

	Average[a]	Rank
Professional Life		
More committed to quality teacher education	3.26	1
Validation as a colleague working with university/college	3.07	2
Renewed enjoyment of/enthusiasm about teaching	3.06	2
Increased respect for university/college faculty	2.89	3
More motivated to invest in the profession	2.37	4
Considering teacher education as a future career	1.89	5
Private Life		
Experienced sense of pride as an individual	2.90	1
More effectively helping people do their own thinking/problem solving	2.80	2
Demonstrating more respect in relationships	2.52	3
Communicating/interacting with others more confidently	2.50	4
Changed attitudes in dealing with family members	1.22	5

SOURCE: Clinard & Ariav (1998, p. 16, table 3).

a. Note: Scale in questionnaire was from 0 ("very little contribution") to 4 ("great contribution"). N:89 (out of 158 participating mentors).

the results of mentor-mentee projects are particularly impressive. See Box 7.1 for mentors' comments about their experiences.

CONCLUSION

When teachers have the autonomy, opportunity, time, and resources to participate in their own and their colleagues' professional growth, instructional improvement is the obvious consequence. The collegial nature of the mentoring relationship, and of the larger mentoring program, means that all involved contribute to its growth and reap its benefits.

Being concerned for others is an important stage in career development. At the utilitarian level, mentors help their own careers by helping others. At the altruistic level, they are like the mentor who said, "I sleep better at night because I do for others what I wish had been done for me!"

> Being a mentor keeps me current. When I have to answer my mentee's questions, it makes me ask, "Why am I doing what I'm doing?" In discussing philosophy, problems, or techniques with this new teacher, I find out what I really believe. That makes me a stronger person and a better teacher. (Gordon & Maxey, 2000, p. 34)

Box 7.1

From the Mentor's Mouth

The following quotations are from teachers experienced with mentoring programs. As these teachers indicate, mentors gain as much or more from their participation as do the beginning teachers.

> *When teachers share their unique talents, there is a sense of electricity in the air. The Mentor Program provides an environment for this excitement to occur. It brings teachers together to share and grow professionally.*

> *I consider it a privilege to work with my colleagues in an exciting, innovative program for teachers.*

> *Teachers learn from students and from each other. I find mentor work stimulating, and it keeps teaching interesting. The stipend for conferences and educational materials keeps me on top of the latest methods, trends, and ideas in teaching.*

> *More than anything, I want to see teachers stay in the profession so they, too, can enjoy the same benefits without the feeling of being lost, or alone, as I did starting out.*

The exchange of ideas helps my teaching. Intellectual discussions with a colleague are stimulating. In helping mentees, I learn more, stay more current. Also, I enjoy the status.

I enjoy working with teachers they're like your best students but even more dedicated and appreciative.

I learn new techniques. It's very beneficial being paired with a recently trained teacher.

I was a new teacher and received tremendous support even though I was very overwhelmed. I truly believe that a support system can help teachers succeed and deal with all the demands of being a new teacher. . . . Collaboration keeps me engaged, interested, and motivated, and I hope to provide that for others.

I am interested in seeing the curriculum that I've developed over the past 25 years continue as a legacy to that mentee and future generations of her students.

I find it very rewarding to work with other teachers [with various levels of experience]. Also, I am dedicated to education, and mentoring offers a unique opportunity to help new teachers.

I get reenergized by working with beginning teachers. I get new ideas and try out new approaches.

SOURCE: Jonson (1999b).

8

Putting It All Together

Come to the edge, he said.
They said: We are afraid.
Come to the edge, he said.
They came.
He pushed them ... and they flew.

—*Guillaume Apollinaire*

There is little doubt that ongoing, meaningful contact between mentors and new teachers reinforces and fosters professional development. The following pages contain a month-by-month calendar of activities designed to promote interaction between these teachers. Activities were selected for each month to correspond with typical events occurring during a school year. Note that this calendar is set up on a traditional schedule, with teachers starting their work of planning in August and beginning in the classroom in September. Adjustments may need to be made for districts where the schedule is year-round or differs in some other way from that presented here.

Activities and topics were selected by reviewing research on the needs of beginning teachers and the experiences reported by mentors and mentees. Mentors and mentees are encouraged to review these activities as a team, to modify them as needed, and to create other activities of their own to maximize the development of their relationship. Activities for school, district, and university involvement, depending on the purposes and extent of the program, are also included. A review of the calendar several months in advance to anticipate needs and plan activities might be useful. Be sure to check the local school, district, and state for requirements and deadlines that need to be incorporated as well. Conference times in individual schools may vary, for example, or statewide testing schedules may need to be incorporated. Jot down any ideas in the process of working through this; room has been left in the calendar for making notes.

Following the month-by-month calendar is a year-at-a-glance checklist. This is a condensed version of the calendar, listing major activities to be checked off. By working together on these activities and others of their own choice, the mentor and mentee will build the trusting relationship that will lead to meaningful teacher development for both.

MONTH-BY-MONTH MENTORING ACTIVITIES

■ **AUGUST**
(or one month prior to start of school)

Mentoring Activities and Ideas

___ **Meet and welcome mentee**.
- Welcome mentee in a telephone call prior to school.
- Take mentee on tour of school building.
- Introduce mentee to other teachers and staff.

___ **Work on developing collegial relationship.**
- Have coffee or lunch away from building.
- Attend social gatherings together or meet in some social setting.

___ **Communicate with principal.**
- Send informal note about making contact with mentee and about initial plans.

School/District/University Activities

___ **Match mentors and mentees.**
___ **Notify mentor-mentee teams of matches.**
___ **Hold orientation or social gathering.**
___ **Schedule workshops.**

Things to Keep in Mind

- Remember: Early contact is essential.
- Establish a system for ongoing communication.
- Orientation or a social gathering is important to success.

■ **SEPTEMBER**
(or first month of school)

Mentoring Activities and Ideas

___ **Hold informal meetings.**
- "Drop in" to touch base with mentee.
- Share a funny or interesting event that happened during the day.
- Write occasional notes acknowledging or supporting mentee's activities and successes.
- Meet informally for coffee.

___ Hold bimonthly conferences to discuss
- Keeping gradebooks
- Maintaining student discipline
- Managing classroom instruction
- Obtaining supplies
- School policies and procedures
- Homework and makeup work policies
- Maximizing academic learning time
- Preparing for parent conferences, contacting parents

___ Help mentee socialize within school.
- Discuss school norms, social traditions.
- Introduce mentee to other staff.
- Show mentee where to find supplies, materials, and so on.
- Review standard operating procedures.

___ Work on collegial relationship with mentee.
- Continue frequent communication and contact.

___ Plan mentor activities with mentee.
- Cooperatively develop flexible Mentor-Mentee Action Plan.

___ Arrange demonstration lesson for mentee.
- Schedule demonstration lesson to be observed and followed up by conference.
- Conduct initial demonstration in mentor's classroom.

___ Communicate with principal.

School/District/University Activities

___ Encourage and support activities.
___ Plan workshops for mentors, mentees, or both.

Things to Keep in Mind

- Be very accessible the first day and week of school.
- Your relationship is key to success.
- Hold at least one scheduled meeting with mentee bimonthly. Focus at meeting on specific ideas and concerns (see specific suggestions for each month).
- "Socialization" includes written and unwritten rules of "how things work around here."
- Tell the school principal about your initial contact and planning with your mentee but *not* about mentee performance.
- Focus on developing a professional, collegial relationship—more than just a friendship.

- See Appendix A for Action Plan examples and forms you can use.
- Refer to "Demonstration Teaching" in Chapter 5 (p. 79) for procedure.
- Have fun!

■ **OCTOBER**
(or second month of school)

Mentoring Activities and Ideas

___ **Hold bimonthly conferences to discuss**
- Parent conferencing, parent contacts
- Report cards
- Classroom management
- Discipline
- Managing instructional tasks, time management
- Audiovisual department
- Student motivation and feedback
- Mentor-Mentee Action Plan

___ **Observe mentee and give feedback.**
- Schedule observation with pre- and postconference time.
- Identify focus for next observation.

___ **Hold informal discussions.**
- Continue to share events and happenings of the day.

___ **Share resources for professional development opportunities, such as**
- State and county offices of education and similar supporting agencies
- Local university and college courses
- District staff development programs

___ **Communicate with principal.**

School/District/University Activities

___ **Plan activities to encourage communication and to allow mentors and mentees to share experiences.**

___ **Consider using principals, district office staff, state and county offices of education, and staff from other supporting agencies in planning mentor-mentee activities.**

Things to Keep in Mind

- The first formal observation should be nonthreatening; refer to "Observation and Feedback" in Chapter 5 (p. 81).
- Consider taking a university class together with your mentee or attending a workshop together.

■ **NOVEMBER**
(or third month of school)

Mentoring Activities and Ideas

___ **Hold bimonthly conferences to discuss**
  - Parent conferences, communications
  - Feedback to students
  - Curriculum resources and materials
  - Mentor-Mentee Action Plan
  - Arrangements for substitute teachers

___ **Continue observation and feedback.**

___ **Continue discussions about professional development opportunities.**

___ **Communicate with principal.**

Things to Keep in Mind

- Check your district and building calendars to anticipate upcoming activities you should discuss or plan for.
- Schedule opportunities for your mentee to observe other teachers. Make suggestions and help with arrangements if appropriate.

■ **DECEMBER**
(or fourth month of school)

Mentoring Activities and Ideas

___ **Hold bimonthly conferences to discuss**
  - School traditions
  - School and district policies regarding holiday events and activities

___ **Communicate informally.**
  - Write short notes of reinforcement and support.

___ **Hold formal observation and conference.**
___ **Communicate with principal.**

Things to Keep in Mind

- Because of holidays, you may not want to do observations this month. Talk it over with your mentee.

■ **JANUARY**
(or fifth month of school)

Mentoring Activities and Ideas

___ **Hold bimonthly conferences to discuss**
- School and classroom procedures for ending and beginning the semester
- Report cards and grading
- Curriculum resources
- Promoting positive relationships among students and teachers
- Mentor-Mentee Action Plan

___ **Review first-term experiences.**
- Discuss highlights.
- Evaluate growth experiences.
- Celebrate successes.

___ **Celebrate completion of first term.**
- Plan visible recognition.

___ **Continue informal communications.**
___ **Communicate with principal.**

School/District/University Activities

___ **Review experiences and evaluate current success of program with mentors or supervisors; identify any modifications needed.**

Things to Keep in Mind

- Reflection helps promote learning and growth.
- Be creative! Involve mentee's students in celebration.
- Informal communications are still very important; look for new opportunities.
- Continue communication with principal.

■ **FEBRUARY**
(or sixth month of school)

Mentoring Activities and Ideas

___ **Hold bimonthly conferences to**
- Plan activities for second semester
- Review and discuss district office staff roles, departments, and support services
- Share literature, research readings, and professional journals
- Review Mentor-Mentee Action Plan
- Discuss use of community resources, such as guest speakers and field trips

___ **Continue informal communications.**
___ **Communicate with principal.**

Things to Keep in Mind

- A plan is very helpful, but it should be reviewed and modified regularly as needs change.
- Be sure to check with the local district and state for mandated test schedules, and build in preparation for tests.

■ **MARCH**
(or seventh month of school)

Mentoring Activities and Ideas

___ **Hold bimonthly conferences to discuss**
- Mentee's concerns and needs
- Professional organizations
- Mentor-Mentee Action Plan

___ **Arrange for mentee observation of other teachers.**
___ **Work on peer-based relationship with mentee.**
___ **Continue informal communications.**
___ **Discuss type of observations needed.**
___ **Communicate with principal.**

School/District/University Activities

___ **Hold inservice workshops for mentors, mentees, or both.**

Things to Keep in Mind

- Your mentee may not be familiar with various professional associations and with the relative advantages of membership.

- Mentees will continue to benefit from observations of other teachers.
- Be *specific* when identifying needs and giving feedback.
- Be sure to make known your own inservice needs and those of other mentors.

■ **APRIL**
(or eighth month of school)

Mentoring Activities and Ideas

___ **Hold bimonthly conferences**.
  - Discuss career planning and development.
  - Talk about testing and evaluation services.
  - Review Mentor-Mentee Action Plan.
  - Begin discussion of bringing the year to a close.

___ **Continue informal communications.**
___ **Continue Action Plan activities.**
___ **Communicate with principal.**

Things to Keep in Mind

- Focus on building the mentee's autonomy and self-confidence.

■ **MAY**
(or ninth month of school)

Mentoring Activities and Ideas

___ **Hold bimonthly conferences**.
  - Discuss procedures for ending the year.
  - Discuss procedures for beginning the following year.

___ **Revise mentor-mentee activities.**
___ **Continue informal communications.**
___ **Build and reinforce peer relationship.**
___ **Communicate with principal.**

School/District/University Activities

___ **Celebrate completion of first year of teaching with**
  - Awards or certificates signed by the superintendent, principal, or director of teacher education program
  - Recognition banquet for mentors and mentees

Things to Keep in Mind

- Begin to move the mentor-mentee relationship away from previously established schedules and patterns.
- Continue to focus on mentee autonomy, self-confidence, and self-direction.
- Review, reflect, and celebrate!

■ **JUNE**
(or final month of school)

Mentoring Activities and Ideas

___ **Hold bimonthly conferences to**
- Discuss mentee concerns
- Review year's events

___ **Continue recognition of mentee and of mentoring program.**
___ **Communicate with principal.**

School/District/University Activities

___ **Evaluate program.**
___ **Identify goals for next year**.

Things to Keep in Mind

- This is a time to reflect on the year just ending and to think of its impact on the year to come.
- The benefits of the program should remain visible to the staff.
- This is a great time for a meeting of all mentors.

YEAR-AT-A-GLANCE CHECKLIST

■ **AUGUST (or one month prior to start of school)**
____   Meet and welcome mentee.
____   Work on developing collegial relationship.
____   Communicate with principal.
____   Begin participation in school/district/university activities.

■ **SEPTEMBER (or first month of school)**
____   Hold informal meetings.
____   Hold bimonthly conferences.
____   Help mentee socialize within school.

_____ Work on collegial relationship with mentee.
_____ Plan mentor activities with mentee.
_____ Arrange demonstration lesson for mentee.
_____ Communicate with principal.

■ **OCTOBER (or second month of school)**
_____ Hold bimonthly conferences.
_____ Observe mentee and give feedback.
_____ Hold informal discussions.
_____ Share resources for professional development opportunities.
_____ Communicate with principal.

■ **NOVEMBER (or third month of school)**
_____ Hold bimonthly conferences.
_____ Continue observation and feedback.
_____ Continue discussions about professional development opportunities.
_____ Communicate with principal.

■ **DECEMBER (or fourth month of school)**
_____ Hold bimonthly conferences.
_____ Communicate informally.
_____ Hold formal observation and conference.
_____ Communicate with principal.

■ **JANUARY (or fifth month of school)**
_____ Hold bimonthly conferences.
_____ Review first-term experiences.
_____ Celebrate completion of first term.
_____ Continue informal communications.
_____ Communicate with principal.

■ **FEBRUARY (or sixth month of school)**
_____ Hold bimonthly conferences.
_____ Continue informal communications.
_____ Communicate with principal.

■ **MARCH (or seventh month of school)**
_____ Hold bimonthly conferences.
_____ Arrange for mentee observation of other teachers.
_____ Work on peer-based relationship with mentee.
_____ Continue informal communications.
_____ Discuss type of observations needed.
_____ Communicate with principal.

■ **APRIL (or eighth month of school)**

____   Hold bimonthly conferences.
____   Continue informal communications.
____   Continue Action Plan activities.
____   Communicate with principal.

■ **MAY (or ninth month of school)**

____   Hold bimonthly conferences.
____   Revise mentor-mentee activities.
____   Continue informal communications.
____   Build and reinforce peer relationship.
____   Communicate with principal.

■ **JUNE (or final month of school)**

____   Hold bimonthly conferences.
____   Continue recognition of mentee and of mentoring program.
____   Communicate with principal.
____   Complete school/district/university activities.

Appendix A

Mentor-Mentee Action Plans

Mentor-Mentee Action Plans can be designed as a collaborative guide for mentors and mentees as they conjointly plan their activities for the academic year. Typically, an Action Plan serves three functions:

1. To clarify the *roles* and *responsibilities* of the mentor and mentee

2. To provide a *focus* and *framework* for mentor-mentee teamwork

3. To becomes an *informative resource* when shared with others

Several sample Mentor-Mentee Action Plans follow. Take a look to see if this sort of planning would work for you. Check with your school or district to see if it has a similar planning form.

Sample (Elementary Level)
Mentor-Mentee Action Plan

Mentor: _____

Mentee: _____

School/District: _____

Date: _____

Three Priority Goals for the Year

I.   To obtain a broad view of teaching styles and strategies

II. To develop mastery of second-grade curriculum

III. To maximize time spent on learning tasks

Objectives	Activity (what, who, where, dates)	Evidence of Completion/Successes
I. Broaden view of styles/strategies. A. Become familiar with three new teaching strategies. B. Attempt use of one new strategy.	Do observation in multiage classrooms (Nov). Take coursework in curriculum integration (10 clock hours Jan/Feb). Have debriefing sessions following observations. Attend workshop Jan 25.	Observed at _____ Elementary School on Nov 9: strategy of guided reading groups Integrated arts into curriculum Viewed instructional videotapes on teaching math with manipulatives (May) Taught thinking skill explicitly
II. Mastery of curriculum A. Build bank of instructional strategies. B. Become familiar with teaching resources.	Locate videos, tapes, and books that support units of study. Obtain list of extended reading materials.	Now know who to contact for resources and know location of many additional materials Implemented alternative strategy that resulted in greater time on learning task Had observations and debriefings that were specific to teaching techniques and student responses

Objectives	Activity (what, who, where, dates)	Evidence of Completion/Successes

III. Time on task
  A. Improve time
    management.
  B. Increase time on
    instructional/learning
    tasks.
	Have observer collect data and provide feedback two times in Oct and Nov.
	
	Brainstorm different management strategies.
	
	Increase mentee's self-awareness of teaching style through self-reflection, observation, feedback, and analysis of data.
		Implemented alternative strategy that resulted in greater time on learning task
		
		Observations and debriefings were specific to teaching techniques and student responses
		
		Students were observed being actively engaged
		
		Increased independent learning and self-study
		
		Completed required units of study
		
		Had positive classroom environment, which resulted in less time spent on discipline and more engaged learning time

Sample (Middle School Level)
Mentor-Mentee Action Plan

Mentor: _____

Mentee: _____

School/District: _____

Date: _____

Three Priority Goals for the Year

I. To become comfortable with the fifth-grade curriculum and find exciting and meaningful ways to present it

II. To gain a general orientation to district and school programs

III. To incorporate cooperative learning as a teaching strategy

Objectives	Activity (what, who, where, dates)	Evidence of Completion/Successes
I. Knowledge of fifth-grade curriculum	A. Weekly Tuesday morning meetings between mentor and mentee to share curriculum materials and instruction techniques B. Mentor and mentee plan a unit to be taught together with combined classes	Ongoing throughout school year Evaluation of unit by mentor and mentee upon completion
II. General orientation	A. Weekly Tuesday morning meetings between mentor and mentee	Ongoing between Sept and June
III. Cooperative learning	A. Videotape two lessons using the cooperative learning teaching strategy	Mentor and mentee observe videotaped lessons together to evaluate

Sample (High School Level)
Mentor-Mentee Action Plan

Mentor: _____

Mentee: _____

School/District: _____

Date: _____

Three Priority Goals for the Year

I.   To use effective educational strategies

II. To coordinate and integrate state, district, and school curriculum standards within the Home and Family Life Program

III. To create a plan for the future direction of the Home and Family Life (HFL) Program and the high school

Objectives	Activity (what, who, where, dates)	Evidence of Completion/Successes
I. A. Become familiar with current, effective, and innovative strategies.	A. 1. Attend Mentor/New Teacher workshop Oct 19.	A. 1. Program, notes, agenda
		A. 2. Training materials, agenda
B. Implement strategies that apply to HFL program at this school.	A. 2 Attend Anti-Smoking Training Oct 16.	A. 3. Note packet
	A. 3. Watch tapes on classroom management.	B. 1. List and evaluation of effectiveness
C. Observe other classrooms.		B. 2. Planbook record
	B. 1. Try techniques and ideas.	C. Calendar record and employee forms
	B. 2. Teach Anti-Smoking Program to ninth graders.	
	C. Observe other teachers within the building (at least three) and in other schools.	

Objectives	Activity (what, who, where, dates)	Evidence of Completion/Successes
II. A. Become familiar with curriculum used at this school. B. Gain an understanding of the high school program. C. Become involved in FHA at district, region, and state levels. D. Become involved in state HFL programs.	A. Review and use FLASH, Family and Futures, and Here's Looking at You. B. 1. Arrange and attend meetings with high school HFL teacher. B. 2. Visit and observe high school HFL and other programs. C. 1. Attend Regional Day and Advisers' Workshop Oct 9. C. 2. Observe HFL program with a well-integrated standards. D. Attend local HFL meetings Oct 28 and Mar 23.	A. Planbook record B. 1. Calendar record of meetings B. 2. Employee leave forms C. 1. Employee leave forms and programs C. 2. Employee leave forms C. 3. Employee leave forms and programs Calendar record
III. A. Explore innovative HFL programs. B. Become familiar with technology and new design within HFL programs.	A. Visit and observe such programs (talk to state supervisor for recommendations). B. Visit and observe programs with new or state-of-the-art designs—for example, the newly remodeled high school.	A. Employee leave forms, notes B. Employee leave forms, notes, and so forth

Appendix B

A Framework of Teaching Competencies

Following is a framework of knowledge, skills, and abilities of effective teachers. Although this sample was designed for and is used in California, most states have something similar to it.

The framework here was developed in 1992 based on a four-year pilot project of the Far West Laboratory for Educational Research and Development (now WestEd, the federal Region XI Comprehensive Assistance Center serving Northern California) for the California Beginning Teacher Support and Assessment (BTSA) program. Its purpose was to enhance the success of new teachers in California by defining a vision of effective beginning teaching and to facilitate the induction of beginning teachers into their professional roles and responsibilities by providing a common language and a new vision of the scope and complexity of teaching. The framework specifies six related dimensions or domains. Together these six standards represent a developmental, holistic view of teaching designed to be used by teachers to

- Prompt reflection about student learning and teaching practice
- Formulate professional goals to improve teaching practice
- Guide, monitor, and assess the progress of a teacher's practice toward professional goals and professionally accepted benchmarks

In July 1997, the State Board of Education adopted this original BTSA framework as the new California Standards for the Teaching Profession, setting forth standards for professional teaching practice in California. The six interrelated categories of teaching competence are as follows:

1. Engaging and Supporting All Students in Powerful Learning. The teacher builds on knowledge of students, subject matter, teaching, and learning to enact effective and powerful learning opportunities with all students. Varied teaching strategies and approaches are used to encourage all students to demonstrate what has been learned in meaningful and authentic ways.

2. Creating and Maintaining an Effective Environment for Student Learning. The teacher creates and maintains a smoothly functioning, safe learning environment in which students assume responsibility for themselves and one another, participate in decision making, work collaboratively and independently, are treated fairly and respectfully, and engage in purposeful learning activities. Student expectations for behavior are clearly established, understood, and consistently maintained. The physical environment and the arrangements within that environment support positive social interactions and facilitate equitable engagement of students in productive tasks.

3. Understanding and Organizing Subject Matter Knowledge for Student Learning. The teacher exhibits strong working knowledge of subject matter content to be taught and is able to use that knowledge to construct meaningful learning activities, products, and long-term projects for all students. Students understand the central themes and concepts within a content area and are able to apply those learnings to other content areas in authentic ways.

4. Planning Instruction and Designing Learning Experiences for All Students. The teacher plans instruction based on knowledge of subject matter, students, and community. The richness of student diversity is reflected in the planning process. Challenging but realistic goals are established for all students, and instructional plans are designed to help students reach those goals.

5. Assessing Student Learning. The teacher establishes and clearly communicates performance expectations and collects information about student performance from a variety of sources. The teacher shares that information with students, parents, and support personnel in ways that improve understanding and foster continued growth and development. The teacher adjusts instruction based on assessment information to ensure enhanced learning opportunities for students.

6. Developing as a Professional Educator. The teacher reflects on his or her own professional development as he or she interacts in a wider learning environment with students, other educators, parents, and community members. The teacher recognizes his or her responsibility to the broader professional community and seeks to learn from and contribute to that community and to improve teaching and learning for all students.

Interested new teachers and mentors should contact the California Department of Education to obtain the complete, updated *California Standards for the Teaching Profession* (or contact the department of education for other states as appropriate). In the *California Standards*, each competency dimension is introduced in a narrative description of best practice that portrays an accomplished level of professional teaching. Following the narrative description, each standard is organized in elements that identify key areas within that domain of teaching. Each element is further specified with questions that encourage teachers to explore aspects of teaching practice throughout their careers. In order to foster ongoing reflection and insights into teaching, the questions are introduced with the stem "How do I . . . ?" The questions can also be phrased as "Why do I . . . ?", which encourages teachers to examine the rationale for key aspects of their teaching.

Appendix C

Teachers' Developmental Stages

Elementary School Level

Teachers can generally be counted on to talk about developmental needs and stages when they discuss children. It may be equally meaningful to think of teachers themselves as having developmental sequences in their professional growth patterns. The purpose of the present discussion is to outline the tasks and associated training needs of each suggested developmental stage and to consider the implications for the timing and location of training efforts.

It seems reasonable to suggest that there may be at least four developmental stages for teachers. Individual teachers may vary greatly in the length of time spent in each of the four stages outlined here.

STAGE 1: SURVIVAL

Developmental Tasks

During this stage, which may last throughout the first full year of teaching, the teacher's main concern is whether or not she can survive. This preoccupation with survival may be expressed in terms like these: "Can I get through the day in one piece? Without losing my patience, my temper, my ideals? Can I make it until the end of the week—the next vacation? Can I really do this kind of work day after day? Will I be accepted by my colleagues?"

The first full impact of responsibility for a group of immature but vigorous students (to say nothing of encounters with their parents) inevitably provokes teacher anxieties. The discrepancy between anticipated successes and classroom realities intensifies feelings of inadequacy and unpreparedness.

Mentoring Needs

During this period, the teacher needs support, understanding, encouragement, reassurance, comfort, and guidance. She needs instruction in specific skills and insight into the complex causes of behavior—all of which must be provided at the classroom site. On-site mentors may be senior staff members, advisers, consultants, or program assistants. Mentoring must be constantly and readily available from someone who knows both the trainee and her teaching situation well. The mentor should have enough time and flexibility to be on call as needed by the trainee. Schedules of periodic visits that have been arranged in advance cannot be counted on to coincide with the mentee's crises.

STAGE II: CONSOLIDATION

Developmental Tasks

By the end of the first year, the teacher has usually decided that she is capable of surviving. She is now ready to consolidate the overall gains made during the first stage and to differentiate specific tasks and skills to be mastered next. During Stage II, teachers usually begin to focus on individual problem students and problem situations. This focus may take the form of looking for answers to such questions as "How can I help a clinging child? How can I help a particular student who does not seem to be learning?"

During Stage I, the neophyte acquires a baseline of information about what students are like and what to expect of them. By Stage II, the teacher is beginning to identify individual students whose behavior departs from the pattern of most of the children she knows.

Mentoring Needs

During this stage, on-site mentoring continues to be valuable. A mentor can help the teacher through mutual exploration of a problem. Take, for example, the case of a young teacher who was eager to get help and expressed her problem in the question, "How should I deal with a clinging child?" An on-site mentor can, of course, observe the teacher and child *in situ* and arrive at suggestions and tentative solution strategies fairly quickly. However, without firsthand knowledge of the child and context, an extended give-and-take conversation between teacher and mentor may be the best way for the mentor to help the teacher to interpret her experience and move toward a solution of the problem. The mentor might ask the teacher such questions as "What have you done so far? Give an example of some experiences with this particular child during this week. When you did such and such, how did the child respond?"

Also, in this stage, the need for information about specific students suggests that learning to use a wider range of resources is needed. Psychologists, social and health workers, and other specialists can strengthen the teacher's skills and knowledge at this time. Exchanges of information and ideas with more experienced colleagues may help teachers master the developmental tasks of this period. Opportunities to share feelings with other teachers in the same stage of development may help to reduce some of the teacher's sense of personal inadequacy and frustration.

STAGE III: RENEWAL

Developmental Tasks

Often, during the third or fourth year of teaching, the teacher begins to tire of doing the same old things. She starts to ask more questions about new developments in the field: "Who is doing what? Where? What are some of the new materials, techniques, approaches, and ideas?" It may be that what the teacher has been doing for each annual crop of students has been quite adequate for them, but she herself finds the recurrent Valentine cards, Easter bunnies, and pumpkin cutouts insufficiently interesting. If it is true that a teacher's own interest or commitment to the projects and activities she provides for children contributes to their educational value, then her need for renewal and refreshment should be taken seriously.

Training Needs

During this stage, teachers find it especially rewarding to meet colleagues from different programs on both formal and informal occasions. Teachers in this developmental stage are particularly receptive to experiences in regional and national conferences and workshops, and they profit from membership in professional associations and participation in their meetings. Teachers are now widening the scope of their reading, scanning numerous magazines and journals, and viewing films. Perhaps during this period they may be ready to take a close look at their own classroom teaching through videotaping. This is also a time when teachers welcome opportunities to visit other classes, programs, and demonstration projects.

Perhaps it is at this stage that the teacher center has the greatest potential value. Teacher centers are places where teachers can gather together to help each other learn or relearn skills, techniques, and methods; to exchange ideas; and to organize special workshops. From time to time, specialists in curriculum, child growth, or any other area of concern that teachers identify are invited to the center to meet with teachers.

STAGE IV: MATURITY

Developmental Tasks

Maturity may be reached by some teachers within three years—in others, in five or more. The teacher at this stage has come to terms with herself as a teacher. She now has enough perspective to begin to ask deeper and more abstract questions, such as "What are my historical and philosophical roots? What is the nature of growth and learning? How are educational decisions made? Can schools change societies? Is teaching a profession?" Perhaps she has asked these questions before. But with the experience she has now gained, the questions represent a more meaningful search for insight, perspective, and realism.

Training Needs

Throughout maturity, teachers need opportunities to participate in conferences and seminars and perhaps to work toward a degree. Mature teachers welcome the chance to read widely and to interact with educators working on many problem areas on many different levels. Training sessions and conference events that Stage II teachers enjoy may be very tiresome to the Stage IV teacher. (Similarly, introspective and searching discussion seminars enjoyed by Stage IV teachers may lead to restlessness and irritability among the beginners of Stage I.)

Summary

Four dimensions of mentoring and training for teaching have been suggested: (a) developmental stages of the teacher, (b) mentoring/training needs of each stage, (c) location of the mentoring/training, and (d) timing of mentoring/training.

1. *Developmental Stages of the Teacher.* It is useful to think of the growth of teachers as occurring in stages that are linked very generally to experience gained over time.

2. *Mentoring/Training Needs of Each Stage.* The mentoring and training needs of teachers change as experience occurs. For example, the issues dealt with in the traditional social foundations of education courses at the university do not seem to address themselves to the early survival problems that are critical to the inexperienced. However, for the maturing

teacher, those same issues may help to deepen her understanding of the total complex context in which she is trying to be effective.

3. *Location of Mentoring/Training.* The location of mentoring/training should be moved as the teacher develops. At the beginning of the new teacher's career, mentoring resources must be taken to her so that mentoring can be responsive to the particular (and possibly unique) developmental tasks and working situation the mentee faces in her classroom. Later on, as the teacher moves past the survival stage, training can move toward the college campus.

4. *Timing of Mentoring/Training.* The timing of mentoring/training should be shifted so that more mentoring and training are available to the teacher on the job than before it. Many teachers say that their preservice education has had only a minor influence on what they do day to day in their classrooms, which suggests that strategies acquired before employment will often not be retrieved under pressure of concurrent forces and factors in the actual job situation.

However, even though it is often said that experience is the best teacher, we cannot assume that experience teaches what the new teacher should learn. To direct this learning, to try to make sure that the beginning teacher has informed and interpreted experience, should be one of the major roles of the teacher-mentor.

SOURCE: Adapted from Katz (1972), "Developmental Stages of Preschool Teachers," *Elementary School Journal, 23*(1): 50-51. Used with permission of the University of Chicago Press.

Appendix D

First-Day Checklist

The first days of school are critical for a new teacher. Harry Wong says that what teachers do on the first days of school determines their success or failure for the rest of the school year (Wong & Wong, 1991). Student achievement at the end of the year is directly related to the degree to which the teacher establishes good control of the classroom procedures in the very first week of the school year. Very few beginning teachers receive any instruction on what to do on the first day of school, and very few get any experience or training during student teaching on what to do on the first day of school.

To prepare for the first day, the beginning teacher often needs help from a mentor. The beginning teacher needs to think through all the specific procedures needed to maintain a classroom environment where instruction and learning can occur. The beginning teacher and mentor can discuss in advance which practices and procedures the beginning teacher will establish and how to communicate these carefully to students so they will know what to expect. The checklist provided here is offered as a discussion starter.

CHECKLIST
Preparing for the First Day

Efficiency in the classroom is the hallmark of an effective learning environment. Established procedures, consistently applied and taught to students at the onset of the school year, will significantly improve classroom management time.

Directions:

- Check each item for which you already have a prepared process.
- Place an X by each item for which you do not have a policy but believe you need one.
- Highlight those items that you will teach the students the first day of class.

I. **Beginning Class**
___ A. Roll call, absent, tardy
___ B. Academic warm-ups
___ C. Distributing materials
___ D. Class opening

II. **Room/School Areas**
___ A. Shared materials
___ B. Teacher's desk
___ C. Drinks, bathroom, pencil sharpener
___ D. Student storage/lockers
___ E. Student desks
___ F. Learning centers, stations
___ G. Playground, school grounds
___ H. Lunchroom
___ I. Halls

III. **Setting Up Independent Work**
___ A. Defining "working alone"
___ B. Identifying problems
___ C. Identifying resources
___ D. Identifying solutions
___ E. Scheduling
___ F. Interim checkpoints

IV. **Instructional Activities**
___ A. Teacher, student contacts
___ B. Student movement in the room
___ C. Signals for students' attention
___ D. Signals for teacher's attention
___ E. Student talk during seatwork
___ F. Activities to do when work is done
___ G. Student participation
___ H. Laboratory procedures
___ I. Movement in and out of small groups
___ J. Bringing materials to school
___ K. Expected behavior in group
___ L. Behavior of students not in group

V. **Ending Class**
___ A. Putting away supplies, equipment
___ B. Cleaning up
___ C. Organizing class materials
___ D. Dismissing class

VI. Interruptions
___ A. Rules
___ B. Talk among students
___ C. Conduct
___ D. Passing out books, supplies
___ E. Turning in work
___ F. Handing back assignments
___ G. Getting back assignments
___ H. Out-of-seat policies
___ I. Consequences for misbehavior

VII. Other Procedures
___ A. Fire drills
___ B. Lunch procedures
___ C. Student helpers
___ D. Safety procedures

VIII. Work Requirements
___ A. Heading papers
___ B. Use of pen or pencil
___ C. Writing on back of paper
___ D. Neatness, legibility
___ E. Incomplete work
___ F. Late work
___ G. Missed work
___ H. Due dates
___ I. Makeup work
___ J. Supplies
___ K. Coloring or drawing on paper
___ L. Use of manuscript or cursive

IX. Communicating Assignments
___ A. Posting assignments
___ B. Orally giving assignments

___ C. Provision for absentees
___ D. Long-term assignments
___ E. Term schedule
___ F. Homework assignments

X. Student Work
___ A. In-class participation
___ B. In-class assignments
___ C. Homework
___ D. Stages of long-term assignments

XI. Checking Assignments in Class
___ A. Students exchanging papers
___ B. Marking and grading assignments
___ C. Turning in assignments
___ D. Students correcting errors

XII. Grading Procedures
___ A. Determining grades
___ B. Recording grades
___ C. Grading long assignments
___ D. Extra-credit work
___ E. Keeping papers, grades, assignments
___ F. Grading criteria
___ G. Contracting for grades

XIII. Academic Feedback
___ A. Rewards and incentives
___ B. Posting student work
___ C. Communicating with parents
___ D. Students' record of grades
___ E. Written comments on assignments

SOURCE: Adapted from *Achieving Excellence*, Mid-Continent Regional Educational Laboratory, Kansas City, MO, 1983.

Appendix E

Supervisory Beliefs Inventory

by Carl Glickman,
Association for Supervision
and Curriculum Development

The Supervisory Beliefs Inventory (Glickman, 1985) is an excellent tool for mentors to use in thinking about the challenges of interpersonal communication and their own personal orientation to supervision. Part I is a prediction section in which individuals guess how they would place themselves. Part II is a forced-choice instrument that, if answered honestly, gives a reality index of how the individual acts. Glickman points out that one orientation is not necessarily better than the others.

For a complete discussion of each of the three orientations, refer to Chapters 3 through 5 in Glickman's *Supervision of Instruction: A Developmental Approach*.

See Chapter 3 in this text for more on Glickman's work. Although he uses the term "supervision," much of what he has to say applies to mentoring.

SOURCE: Glickman, C. D. (1985). *Supervision of instruction: A developmental approach.* Alexandria, VA: Association for Supervision and Curriculum Development.
From "Developmental Supervision: Alternative Practices for Helping Teachers Improve Instruction," by Carl D. Glickman, 1981, pp. 12-15. Alexandria, VA: Association for Supervision and Curriculum Development. Copyright © 1981 ASCD. Reprinted by permission. All rights reserved.

THE SUPERVISORY BELIEFS INVENTORY

This inventory is designed for supervisors to assess their own beliefs about teacher supervision and professional development. The inventory assumes that supervisors believe and act according to all three of the orientations of supervision, yet one usually dominates. The inventory is designed to be self-administered and self-scored. The second part lists items for which supervisors must choose one of two options. A scoring key follows, which can be used to compare the predictions of Part I with the actual beliefs indicated by the forced-choice items of Part II.

Part I. Predictions

Instructions: Check one answer for each question.

	Percent of Time				
Questions	*Nearly 100%*	*About 75%*	*About 50%*	*About 20%*	*About 0%*
1. How often do you use a *directive approach* (rather than one of the other two approaches) in supervising teachers?	_____	_____	_____	_____	_____
2. How often do you use a *collaborative approach* (rather than one of the other two approaches) in supervising teachers?	_____	_____	_____	_____	_____
3. How often do you use a *nondirective approach* (rather than one of the other two approaches) in supervising teachers?	_____	_____	_____	_____	_____

Part II. Forced Choices

Instructions: Circle either A or B for each item. You may not completely agree with either choice, but choose the one that is closest to how you feel.

1. A. Supervisors should give teachers a large degree of autonomy and initiative within broadly defined limits.
   B. Supervisors should give teachers directions about methods that will help them improve their teaching.

2. A. It is important for teachers to set their own goals and objectives for professional growth.
   B. It is important for supervisors to help teachers reconcile their personalities and teaching styles with the philosophy and direction of the school.

3. A. Teachers are likely to feel uncomfortable and anxious if the objectives on which they will be evaluated are not clearly defined by the supervisor.
   B. Evaluations of teachers are meaningless if teachers are not able to define with their supervisors the objectives for evaluation.

4. A. An open, trusting, warm, and personal relationship with teachers is the most important ingredient in supervising teachers.
   B. A supervisor who is too intimate with teachers risks being less effective and less respected than a supervisor who keeps a certain degree of professional distance from teachers.

5. A. My role during supervisory conferences is to make the interaction positive, to share realistic information, and to help teachers plan their own solutions to problems.
   B. The methods and strategies I use with teachers in a conference are aimed at our reaching agreement over the needs for future improvement.

6. In the initial phase of working with a teacher:
   A. I develop objectives with each teacher that will help accomplish school goals.
   B. I try to identify the talents and goals of individual teachers so they can work on their own improvement.

7. When several teachers have a similar classroom problem, I prefer to:
   A. Have the teachers form an ad hoc group and help them work together to solve the problem.
   B. Help teachers on an individual basis find their strengths, abilities, and resources so that each one finds his or her own solution to the problem.

8. The most important clue that an inservice workshop is needed is when:

A. The supervisor perceived that several teachers lack knowl-edge of skill in a specific area, which is resulting in low morale, undue stress, and less effective teaching.

B. Several teachers perceive the need to strengthen their abilities in the same instructional area.

9. A. The supervisory staff should decide the objectives of an inser-vice workshop since they have a broad perspective of the teachers' abilities and the school's needs.

B. Teachers and the supervisory staff should reach consensus about the objectives of an inservice workshop before the workshop is held.

10. A. Teachers who feel they are growing personally will be more effective in the classroom than teachers who are not experi-encing personal growth.

B. The knowledge and ability of teaching strategies and methods that have been proven over the years should be taught and practiced by all teachers to be effective in their classrooms.

11. When I perceive that a teacher might be scolding a student unnecessarily:

A. I explain, during a conference with the teacher, why the scold-ing was excessive.

B. I ask the teacher about the incident but do not interject my judgment.

12. A. One effective way to improve teacher performance is to for-mulate clear behavioral objectives and create meaningful incentives for achieving them.

B. Behavioral objectives are rewarding and helpful to some teachers but stifling to others; also, some teachers benefit from behavioral objectives in some situations but not in others.

13. During a preobservation conference:

A. I suggest to the teacher what I could observe, but I let the teacher make the final decision about the objectives and meth-ods of observation.

B. The teacher and I mutually decide the objectives and methods of observation.

14. A. Improvement occurs very slowly if teachers are left on their own, but when a group of teachers works together on a spe-cific problem, they learn rapidly and their morale remains high.

B. Group activities may be enjoyable, but I find that individual, open discussion with a teacher about a problem and its possi-ble solutions leads to more sustained results.

15. When an inservice or professional development workshop is scheduled:

A. All teachers who participated in the decision to hold the work-shop should be expected to attend it.

B.   Teachers, regardless of their role in forming a workshop, should be able to decide if the workshop is relevant to their personal or professional growth and, if not, should not be expected to attend.

Scoring Key

Step 1. Circle your answer from Part II of the inventory in the columns below.

Column I	Column II	Column III
1B	1A	
	2B	2A
3A	3B	
4B		4A
	5B	5A
6A		6B
	7A	7B
8A		8B
9A	9B	
10B		10A
11A		11B
12A	12B	
	13B	13A
14B	14A	
	15A	15B

Step 2. Tally the total number of circled items in each column and multiply by 6.7.

2.1 Total response in Column I   _____X 6.7 = _____
2.2 Total response in Column II   _____X 6.7 = _____
2.3 Total response in Column III _____X 6.7 = _____

Step 3. Interpretation

The product you obtained in Step 2.1 is an approximate percentage of how often you take a directive approach to supervision, rather than either of the other two approaches. The product you obtained in Step 2.2 is an approximate percentage of how often you take a collaborative approach to supervision, rather than either of the other two approaches, and the product you obtained in Step 2.3 is an approximate percentage of how often you take a nondirective approach. The approach on which you spend the greatest percentage of time is the supervisory model that dominates your beliefs. If the percentage values are equal or close to equal, you take an eclectic approach.

You can also compare these results with your predictions in Part I.

What to Do With Your Score

You now have a base to look at the orientation with which you are most comfortable. If your scores for two or three orientations were about equal (30% nondirective, 40% collaborative, and 30% directive), you are either confused or more positively eclectic. If you are eclectic, you probably consider varying your supervisory orientations according to each situation. Practitioners of one orientation might be more effective by learning the very precise supervisory behaviors that are needed to make that orientation work. To think that supervision is collaborative is incomplete until one knows how to employ techniques that result in collaboration. Many supervisors and mentors profess to be of a certain orientation but unknowingly use behaviors that result in different outcomes.

References

Acheson, J., & Gall, M. (1980). *Techniques in the clinical supervision of teachers*. New York: Longman.

Albert, S., Blondino, C., & McGrath, J. (1990). *Peer coaching*. Seattle, WA: Puget Sound Educational Service District.

Association for Supervision and Curriculum Development. (1999a). *Mentoring to improve schools: Facilitator's guide*. Alexandria, VA: Author.

Association for Supervision and Curriculum Development. (1999b). *Mentoring to improve schools: Successful mentoring programs* [Videotape]. Alexandria, VA: Author.

Association for Supervision and Curriculum Development. (1999c). Preparing two million: How districts and states attract and retain teachers. *Education Update, 41*(1), 1.

Bacon, D. (1997, October 6). Veteran teachers lend a hand: Peer Assistance and Review Program celebrates ten years. *California Teacher, 1*, 6-7.

Bartell, C. (1995). Shaping teacher induction policy in California. *Teacher Education Quarterly, 22*(4), 27-43.

Bey, T. M. (1992). Mentoring in teacher education: Diversifying support for teachers. In T. M. Bey & C. T. Holmes (Eds.), *Mentoring: Contemporary principles and issues* (pp. 111-120). Reston, VA: Association of Teacher Educators.

Bolton, E. (1980). A conceptual analysis of the mentor relationship in the career development of women. *Adult Education, 30*, 195-297.

Bova, B. (1987). Mentoring as a learning experience. In V. J. Marsick (Ed.), *Learning in the workplace*. London: Croom Helm.

Bova, B. M., & Phillips, R. R. (1983). Mentoring as a learning experience for adults. *Journal of Teacher Education, 35*(3), 16-20.

Brennan, S., Thames, W., & Roberts, R. (1999). In Kentucky: Mentoring with a mission. *Educational Leadership, 56*(8), 49-52.

Brookfield, S. D. (1986). *Understanding and facilitating adult learning*. San Francisco: Jossey-Bass.

Brown, M. H., & Williams, A. (1977). Lifeboat ethics and the first year teacher. *Clearinghouse, 51*, 73.

Bullough, R. V. (1990). Supervision, mentoring, and self-discovery: A case study of a first year teacher. *Journal of Curriculum and Supervision, 5*, 338-360.

Bush, R. N. (1996). The formative years. In *The real world of beginning teachers* (pp. 1-14). Washington, DC: National Education Foundation.

Christenbury, L. (1995). Breaking the silence. *A Word to the Wise, 1*(2), 3.

Clinard, L. M., & Ariav, T. (1998, Spring). What mentoring does for mentors: A cross-cultural perspective. *European Journal of Teacher Education, 21*(1), 91-108.

Cohen, N. H. (1995). *Mentoring adult learners: A guide for educators and trainers.* Malabar, FL: Krieger.

Commission on Teacher Credentialing. (1991). "I was really nervous, but I learned a lot": New developments in the CNTP assessment component. *Teacher News, 3*(2), 1-7.

Costa, A. L., & Garmston, R. J. (1994). *Cognitive coaching: A foundation for renaissance schools.* Norwood, MA: Christopher-Gordon.

Costa, A. L., & Kallick, B. (2000). Getting into the habit of reflection. *Educational Leadership, 57*(7), 60-62.

Daloz, L. A. (1999). *Mentor: Guiding the journey of adult learners.* San Francisco: Jossey-Bass.

Darling-Hammond, L. (1988). The futures of teaching. *Educational Leadership, 46*(3), 4-10.

Developmental Studies Center. (1998). *The master teacher handbook.* Unpublished manuscript.

Doyle, W. (1990). Classroom knowledge as a foundation for teaching. *Teachers College Record, 91,* 347-360.

Farkas, S., Johnson, J., & Foleno, T. (2000). *A sense of calling: Who teaches and why.* New York: Public Agenda.

Feiman-Nemser, S. (1996). Teacher mentoring: A critical review. *Peer Resources.* Retrieved November 30, 2001, from www.islandnet.com/~rcarr/teacher-mentors.html

Fraser, J. (1998). *Teacher to teacher: A guidebook for effective mentoring.* Portsmouth, NH: Heinemann.

Galvez-Martin, M. E., Bowman, C., & Morrison, M. (1999). *ATE Newsletter, 32*(6), 4.

Gandal, M., & Vranek, J. (2001). Standards: Here today, here tomorrow. *Educational Leadership, 59*(31), 6-13.

Glatthorn, A. A. (1984). *Differential supervision.* Alexandria, VA: Association for Supervision and Curriculum Development.

Glickman, C. D. (1985). *Supervision of instruction: A developmental approach.* Alexandria, VA: Association for Supervision and Curriculum Development.

Goodlad, J. I. (1984). *A place called school: Prospects for the future.* New York: McGraw-Hill.

Gordon, S. P., & Maxey, S. (2000). *How to help beginning teachers succeed.* Alexandria, VA: Association for Supervision and Curriculum Development.

Gray, W. A., & Gray, M. M. (1985). Synthesis of research on mentoring beginning teachers. *Educational Leadership, 43*(3), 37-38.

Gursky, D. (2000). Supply and demand: Finding and training the teachers we need for the 21st century. *On Campus, 20*(4), 10-12, 15.

Guskey, T. R. (2000). *Evaluating professional development.* Thousand Oaks, CA: Corwin Press.

Haberman, M. (1987). *Recruiting and selecting teachers for urban schools*. Reston, VA: Association of Teacher Educators and ERIC Clearinghouse on Urban Education.

Hardcastle, B. (1988). Spiritual connections: Proteges' reflections on significant mentorships. *Theory Into Practice, 27,* 201-208.

Harrington, T. (2001, July 19). Teacher learns tough lesson in first year. *Concord Transcript, The Contra Costa Times,* pp. 1, 5.

Huling-Austin, L. (1987). Teacher induction. In D. M. Brooks (Ed.), *Teacher induction: A new beginning*. Reston, VA: Association of Teachers and Educators.

Huling-Austin, L. (1988, April). *A synthesis of research on teacher induction programs and practices*. Paper presented at the annual meeting of the American Educational Research Association, New Orleans, LA. (ERIC Document Reproduction Service No. ED302546)

Huling-Austin, L. (1992). Research on learning to teach: Implications for teacher induction and mentoring programs. *Journal of Teacher Education, 43,* 173-180.

Hunter, M. (1994). *Enhancing teaching*. New York: Macmillan.

Jonson, K. (1997). *The new elementary teacher's handbook: (Almost) everything you need to know for your first years of teaching*. Thousand Oaks, CA: Corwin.

Jonson, K. (1998). Providing a safety net for new teachers: University-school district collaboration. *Academic Exchange Quarterly, 2*(2), 21-28.

Jonson, K. (1999a). Parents as partners: Building positive home-school relationships. *The Educational Forum, 63,* 121-126.

Jonson, K. (1999b). [Survey of 28 mentor-teachers in the San Francisco Unified School District]. Unpublished raw data.

Joyce, B., & Showers, B. (1982). The coaching of teaching. *Educational Leadership, 40*(1), 4-12.

Joyce, B., & Showers, B. (1983). *Power in staff development through research on training*. Alexandria, VA: Association for Supervision and Curriculum Development.

Joyce, B., & Showers, B. (1995). *Student achievement through staff development*. White Plains, NY: Longman.

Katz, L. (1972). Developmental stages of preschool teachers. *Elementary School Journal, 23*(1), 50-51.

Kay, R. S. (1990). Mentoring: Definition, principles, and applications. In T. M. Bey & C. T. Holmes (Eds.), *Mentoring: Developing successful new teachers*. Reston, VA: Association of Teacher Educators.

Knowles, M. S. (1980). *The modern practice of adult education: From pedagogy to andragogy*. River Grove, IL: Follett.

Kram, K. E. (1985). *Mentoring at work*. Glenview, IL: Scott Foresman.

Levine, A. (1999, April 7). Dueling goals for education. *New York Times,* p. A21.

Levine, S. L. (1989). *Promoting adult growth in schools*. Needham Heights, MA: Allyn & Bacon.

Levinson, D. (1986). *Seasons of a man's life*. New York: Knopf.

Lortie, D. C. (1975). *Schoolteacher: A sociological study*. Chicago: University of Chicago Press.

Losing sleep. (2001, January 23). *Contra Costa Times,* sec. D.

Lou Harris & Associates. (1991). *The Metropolitan Life Survey of the American Teacher, 1991. The first year: New teachers' expectations and ideals*. New York: Author.

Marsick, V. J. (Ed.). (1987). *Learning in the workplace*. New York: Croom Helm.

Mathison, C. (1996). The challenges of beginning middle and secondary urban school teachers. *Issues in Teacher Education, 5*(1), 5-18.

McGreal, T. L. (1983). *Successful teacher evaluation.* Alexandria, VA: Association for Supervision and Curriculum Development.

Means, B. (2000). Technology in America's schools: Before and after Y2K. In R. S. Brandt (Ed.), *Education in a new era.* Alexandria, VA: Association for Supervision and Curriculum Development.

Mid-Continent Regional Educational Laboratory. (1983). *Time management.* Kansas City, MO: Author.

Moir, E. (1999). The stages of a teacher's first year. In M. Scherer (Ed.), *A better beginning: Supporting and mentoring new teachers.* Alexandria, VA: Association for Supervision and Curriculum Development.

Moran, S. (1990). Schools and the beginning teacher. *Phi Delta Kappan, 72,* 210-213.

Murray, M. (1991). *Beyond the myths and magic of mentoring.* San Francisco: Jossey-Bass.

Northwest Regional Educational Laboratory. (1986). *Training model for academic efficiency.* Developed under contract with the Washington State Superintendent of Public Instruction, Olympia, WA.

Odell, S. J. (1990). Support for new teachers. In T. M. Bey & C. T. Holmes (Eds.), *Mentoring: Developing successful new teachers* (pp. 3-23). Reston, VA: Association of Teacher Educators.

O'Neil, J. (1993). Supervision reappraised. *ASCD Update, 35*(6), 1, 3, 8.

Orlich, D. C. (1989). *Staff development: Enhancing human potential.* Boston: Allyn & Bacon.

Pearson, M. J., & Honig, B. (1992). Problems confronting beginning teachers. In *Success for beginning teachers: The California New Teacher Project* (pp. 5-14). Sacramento: California Department of Education, California Commission on Teacher Credentialing.

Portner, H. (1998). *Mentoring new teachers.* Thousand Oaks, CA: Corwin.

Portner, H. (2001). *Training mentors is not enough.* Thousand Oaks, CA: Corwin.

President Clinton's Call to Action for American Education in the 21st Century. (1997). Retrieved February 8, 2002, from www.ed.gov/updates/PresEDPlan

Raspberry, W. (2000). Lessons teachers beg to be taught. *ATE Newsletter, 33*(4), 3.

Roche, G. R. (1979). Much ado about mentors. *Harvard Business Review, 57*(1), 14-16, 20, 24-27.

Rowley, J. B. (1999). The good mentor. *Educational Leadership, 56*(8), 20-22.

Ryan, K. (1986). *The induction of new teachers* (Phi Delta Kappa Fastback No. 237). Bloomington, IN: Phi Delta Kappa Educational Foundation.

Sacks, S. R., & Brady, P. (1985, March-April). *Who teaches the city's children? A study of New York City first year teachers.* Paper presented at the annual meeting of the American Educational Research Association, Chicago.

Scherer, M. (Ed.). (1999). *A better beginning.* Alexandria, VA: Association for Supervision and Curriculum Development.

Scherer, M. (2001). Making standards work. *Educational Leadership, 1*(1), 5.

Schlechty, P. C., & Vance, V. S. (1983). Recruitment, selection, and retention: The shape of the teaching force. *Elementary School Journal, 83,* 469-487.

Schultz, B. (1999). Combining mentoring and assessment in California. In M. Scherer (Ed.), *A better beginning: Supporting and mentoring new teachers.* Alexandria, VA: Association for Supervision and Curriculum Development.

Sergiovanni, T. J. (1992). Collegiality as a professional virtue. In *Moral leadership: Getting to the heart of school improvement*. San Francisco: Jossey-Bass

Shanker, A. (1995, February 22). *Sink or swim*. Retrieved February 8, 2002, from www.aft.org/stand/previous/1995/012295.html

Showers, B. (1985, April). Teachers coaching teachers. *Educational Leadership, 42*(7), 43-48.

Shulman, J. H., & Colbert, J. A. (Eds.). (1988). *The intern teacher casebook*. San Francisco: Far West Laboratory for Educational Research and Development.

Smith, R. D. (1993). Mentoring new teachers: Strategies, structures, and successes. *Teacher Education Quarterly, 20*(4), 5-18.

Stanulis, R. N., & Weaver, D. (1998). Teacher as mentor, teacher as learner: Lessons from a middle-school language arts teacher. *The Teacher Educator, 34*(2), 134-143.

Teacher voices: The beginning teacher project. (1996). *Newsletter of Beginning Teacher Induction Network, 1*(3), 3.

U.S. Department of Education. (1997). *Seven priorities of the U.S. Department of Education* (Working document). Retrieved February 8, 2002, from www.ed.gov/updates/7priorities

Varah, L. J., Theune, W. S., & Parker, L. (1986). Beginning teachers: Sink or swim? *Journal of Teacher Education, 37*(1), 30-33.

Watson, J., workshop facilitator. Teacher Assistance Program (T.A.P.) conference, Educational Service District, Seattle, WA, January 11, 1992.

Wilson, B., Ireton, E., & Wood, J. (1997). Beginning teacher fears. *Education, 117*, 380, 396-400.

Wong, H. K., & Wong, R. T. (1991). *The first days of school: How to be an effective teacher*. Sunnyvale, CA: Harry K. Wong.

Zachary, L. J. (2000). *The mentor's guide: Facilitating effective learning relationships*. San Francisco, CA: Jossey-Bass.

Zey, M. G. (1984). *The mentor connection*. Homewood, IL: Dow Jones-Irwin.

Zimpher, N. L., & Grossman, J. E. (1992). Collegial support by teacher mentors and peer consultants. In C. D. Glickman (Ed.), *Supervision in transition: 1992 yearbook of the Association for Supervision and Curriculum Development* (pp. 141-154). Alexandria, VA: Association for Supervision and Curriculum Development.

Index